A Beautiful Season

A Beautiful Season

FINDING YOUR IDENTITY IN CHRIST
AFTER A DATING RELATIONSHIP ENDS

ALEXANDRA J. SAVAGE

AMBASSADOR INTERNATIONAL
GREENVILLE, SOUTH CAROLINA & BELFAST, NORTHERN IRELAND

www.ambassador-international.com

A Beautiful Season
Finding your Identity in Christ after a Dating Relationship Ends

ISBN: 978-1-62020-547-1
eISBN: 978-1-62020-455-9

Cover Design and Page Layout by Hannah Nichols
eBook Conversion by Anna Riebe Raats

AMBASSADOR INTERNATIONAL
Emerald House
427 Wade Hampton Blvd.
Greenville, SC 29609, USA
www.ambassador-international.com

AMBASSADOR BOOKS
The Mount
2 Woodstock Link
Belfast, BT6 8DD, Northern Ireland, UK
www.ambassadormedia.co.uk

The colophon is a trademark of Ambassador

To my beautiful mother, Amy—my prayer warrior,

my role model, and one of my best friends.

CONTENTS

INTRODUCTION   9

CHAPTER ONE
WENDY'S RETURN FROM NEVERLAND   15

CHAPTER TWO
LET IT GO!   23

CHAPTER THREE
'TIS THE SEASON   33

CHAPTER FOUR
CUBIC ZIRCONIA VS. DIAMOND   47

CHAPTER FIVE
BEAUTIFUL THINGS   53

CHAPTER SIX
BUILD A BOAT   69

CHAPTER SEVEN
TRAINING YOUR EAR   79

CHAPTER EIGHT
FROG   87

CHAPTER NINE
PRAYER WARRIORS   97

CHAPTER TEN
P31 WOMEN   107

CHAPTER ELEVEN
ETERNAL FOOTPRINTS   113

CHAPTER TWELVE
THE KIND OF LOVE THAT WE DESERVE   125

CHAPTER THIRTEEN
YELLOW LEAVES   133

ABOUT THE AUTHOR   143

INTRODUCTION

No test or temptation that comes your way is beyond the
course of what others have had to face. All you need to remember is that God will never let you down; he'll never let
you be pushed past your limit; he'll always be there to help
you come through it.

1 Corinthians 10:13 (MSG)

HOPE IS AN UNDERLYING MESSAGE of the Bible. Notice the words,
"He'll always be there to help you come through it." God isn't sometimes there for us; He's always there for us. This holds true for what
you are going through and experiencing today. God will always help
us get through the rough patches of life. This includes breakups and
being single. While I am not saying that singleness is a rough patch,
what I am saying is that you may still be hurting and that is okay.
Given the right ingredients, our outlook and the perspective of our
circumstance can be changed. With the help of Jesus Christ, we can
learn how to be joyful regardless of our circumstances.

I don't like the idea of a "broken heart." No one should ever be
allowed to claim the title of "heartbreaker" or even be able to say, "I
broke his or her heart." In this book, you will not hear those phrases

9

being referred to. For followers of Christ, only God deserves to have authority over our hearts. Never give someone or yourself the prideful idea that people have the ability to break hearts. Having this mentality will only lead you to emotional destruction and despair. Moping around and claiming that you are "brokenhearted" can be dangerous because it can inhibit spiritual growth. In a way, giving someone this kind of a seat in your life, and the authority over your happiness, is idolatry. God Himself should be number one in our hearts. This is so that if you and a significant other do break up, the Holy Spirit has been and will remain in full control of your life, your emotions, and your spiritual wellbeing. Repeat these words: *I will allow no one to* "*break my heart." God alone has full control.*

As an author, I am very fond of the concept that you can only write about what you know. I was in a serious dating relationship that lasted for three years before I realized and accepted that God had something greater in mind for my life. Overcoming my past relationship with the help of Jesus Christ and the support of Christian women in my life is a major part of my testimony. By having Jesus as the backboard during my rebound, God used a challenging life experience to shape me into the woman I am today. I hope that as you are going through a similar, tough experience that your testimony will be strengthened and that you will be able to say and believe, "I have been changed for the better." I hope you will realize that there is hope after a breakup, there is beauty in singleness, and there is joy in today.

"Place God above all else and he will meet your every need" (Matthew 6:33). Jesus is in my heart, He is ever present in my life, He knows my every thought, and He recognizes my every need. Jeremiah 29:11 sheds light on a simple biblical truth that is so often overlooked: "For I know the plans I have for you declares The Lord; plans to prosper and not to harm you, plans to give you hope and a future." We recite this verse and memorize it, but do we always believe what God is telling us here? Having faith in God's plan is essential to discovering the purposes for our lives. By trusting in God's plan, we enable Him to do great works through us. Faith is the key that unlocks the door for God to pour out endless possibilities and unimaginable blessings in our lives. Throughout the pages of this book we are going to be searching for this important key. The key of faith holds great power, but also comes with a price.

As Christians, we are called to pick up our cross and follow Jesus daily. Jesus is the essence of our faith. He is the Way, the Truth, and the Life. No one comes to the Father, except through Jesus (John 14:6). By learning from Him, we can grow spiritually and find the key of faith. With Jesus on our side, our faith can become so strong that it has the power to move mountains, and to heal our hurt. Through our every circumstance, may we seek the key holder of our faith, Jesus Christ.

But what does it mean to "seek the key holder of our faith"? There are so many different ways that we can be Jesus' hands and feet to the world. Being a Christ follower looks different for everyone. By discovering who we are and finding our identity in Christ, we are better able to reach others and spread God's love.

My mom always gave me great advice on dating in the form of two short words—"never settle." Ask God for wisdom to recognize what His plans are for you. If you are currently in a relationship that is not God's best for you then do not procrastinate on gracefully ending things. I consider myself blessed to have ended my serious relationship before we stepped past the point of no return—marital union. If you know he is not the one, then don't waste your time. One author put it this way, "When someone brings more problems to your life than happiness, it's time to show them the door where they can exit" (Anonymous). This seems like common sense, but so often love is blind. The Bible offers this advice: "Listen to advice and accept instruction, and in the end you will be wise" (Proverbs 19:20). We need to make the choice to listen to other people's advice because the Bible says so! By remaining in the wrong relationship, you run the risk of missing the right one when he comes along. In the scheme of life, being single is a short season. It's much better to realize that you and your significant other are not right for each other before the wedding bells ring, rather than after. Divorce is a messy, no fun, expensive, and emotionally draining process (so I've been told). Make yourself open, and available now, to the one God has in mind, the man of your dreams.

The Lord works in mysterious ways. May you become closer to Jesus through this experience, and realize that His love is the greatest comfort. By teaching ourselves to depend upon Christ for our heart's needs, we become strong, confident women of God. Women of God are fortified in their faith, relying on Him for all understanding. Women of God are confident in themselves. Women of God are intentional about sharing the message of hope and joy that is found in Jesus Christ. However, there is a disclaimer. Women of God sometimes fail to do these things, mess up, and sin. Throughout the chapters of this book, I am going to become 100 percent transparent, revealing pieces of my past, the places where I have messed up and have fallen short of the glory of God. By God's grace I am forgiven. This book is a culmination of things that I have learned from my past and even current experiences. I hope the words of this book will encourage you, and help you to move forward in faith. I hope the following pages help drown out some of the lies Satan is feeding you, and make you realize that you are not alone in your struggles. I hope the uplifting messages from this book enable you to be confident in yourself. Most of all, I hope God uses this book to empower you to run the race in such a way that you might receive the prize (1 Corinthians 9:24).

While enjoying the pages of this book, remember that what you are reading is superfluous and separate from the Bible. In order to get the full benefits from reading this book, I strongly encourage you to look up the verses I reference, which are in parentheses. The Bible is the book of true wisdom, the main source you should consider when looking for answers directly from God. *A Beautiful Season* and the Bible are two separate entities. While my goal is to provide biblically sound advice, and I prayed every day while writing this book that God would give me the words to write, this book is not the Word of God. Please, please don't substitute this book for the Bible. I have been guilty of this myself when it comes to neglecting some of my time spent in the Word because I am really enjoying reading a particular Christian self-help book. Although self-help books may offer refreshing, new perspectives on life circumstances, godly wisdom comes solely from the Bible. His book is the real deal, the best self-help book available that is applicable to every life situation. I pray that *A Beautiful Season* will encourage you in what you are going through.

Ultimately, however, I pray that the Word will be your main source of hope and light through this season.

Every woman has a story. Every woman has a past. Every woman has a purpose. God has been divinely designing our lives all along. Through Christian counseling, prayer, and reading God's Word, I have discovered the exciting truth that my story is really God's story playing out in my life (Ephesians 4:1). In allowing God to use our pain for His plans, we allow God to turn our past into our purpose. May our testimonies ring the truth: our past, future, and even current circumstances are not our identity. Jesus Christ is our sole identity!

CHAPTER ONE

WENDY'S RETURN FROM NEVERLAND

YOU 'RE CLIMBING A MOUNTAIN. You have almost reached the top, but wait a second! You have to turn around immediately and climb back down. The breakup experience is similar to coming close to reaching the peak of a mountaintop, but for some reason or another having to turn back around just before accomplishing the feat.

"Woke up late today, and I still feel the sting of the pain, but I brushed my teeth anyway, got dressed through the mess and put a smile on my face." As the lyrics from the Sara Evans song, "A Little Bit Stronger" played on my radio, I bawled my eyes out. A breakup can be one of the worst life experiences, but only if you let it. There are ways to cope with the pain that are healthy, and some that are not. I know this because I was in a three-year relationship when God closed the door to what I thought was supposed to last forever. The initial devastation that I experienced was almost too much to bear, until I chose to look for the window of hope that God provided for me. As a result of Jesus' relentless love, my life echoes the anthem of 1 Corinthians 10:13, when God promises His people that they will never encounter a trial that they are not able to endure and overcome through the strength of Jesus Christ.

> No test or temptation that comes your way is beyond the course of what others have had to face. All you need to remember is that God will never let you down; he'll never let you be pushed past your limit; he'll always be there to help you come through it.
>
> — 1 Corinthians 10:13 (MSG)

Did you ever think you are like Wendy from *Peter Pan?* Your answer may be a resounding no, but if we look at Wendy's life and her story, we may find that in a way, as women, we share a lot in common with her. Wendy is just an innocent little girl whose parents want her to grow up and become a lady. She is totally unaware that a whole other world of adventure and wonder exists until Peter steps into her life. Yes, we all have had a Peter in our lives. Peter Pan is the boy who comes to England from Neverland and literally sweeps Wendy off her feet. Together they fly away to Neverland, a magical land of pirates, fairies, and enchantment. Wendy meets Peter's gang of friends, The Lost Boys, and experiences new things in life for the first time. Each day spent with Peter Pan is filled with happiness and adventure. He is a warrior who not only sticks up for Wendy, but also protects her from Captain Hook. Yes, Peter Pan is dreamy. He is the leader of the pack. Like a little lost puppy, Wendy follows Peter around, wherever the wind takes him. Wendy hates Tinker Bell, the cute little fairy who also happens to follow Peter. She gets so jealous of Tink and Peter's tight-knit friendship. Wendy experiences the greatest adventures of her life up until that point with Peter Pan in Neverland. But eventually, Wendy becomes homesick. She misses her family, her friends, and her life back in England, and decides she must go home. She realizes that growing up is an integral part of life, and that she must become the woman she was born to be. Returning home, Wendy stops striving to become Peter Pan's Wendy, and instead seeks her true identity as a young lady, a daughter, and an older sister. Still, the memories Wendy shared with Peter, she will always have and hold dear to her heart. Peter Pan returns to Wendy's house in England several times, but with each reunion, Wendy grows older. Eventually Wendy gets married. She has children and even grandchildren of her own. One last time Peter Pan returns to visit Wendy, and the window is forever shut.

While attending the University of Tulsa, I had a great college experience. But, I struggled with maintaining purity, and living a lifestyle that was glorifying to God. My junior year of college the freshman track star stepped into my life. We began dating and I quickly fell in love. I made so many wonderful memories with him throughout college, but there were also many perilous, terrifying memories tattooed on my past life as well. My ex-boyfriend had anger issues. There were many instances where he became enraged with jealousy over something stupid that most guys wouldn't even notice. There would be screaming, yelling, and belittling comments exchanged between us. It was a harmful relationship, but for some reason or another I was always justifying the bad things that happened in our relationship. I believed the Devil's lies that this was all that I really deserved, and didn't want to end up alone.

My dad did not like my boyfriend at the time from day one. When we were moving my brother Tate, who also went to TU, across campus to a new apartment, my dad needed help moving a couch. Keep in mind, this was the first time my new boyfriend was meeting my parents. My dad asked for help moving the couch and my ex-boyfriend actually told my dad that he couldn't help because he had a fraternity meeting to go to. Wow, way to impress my parents. Of course, I wasn't thinking about it clearly at the time. I was always making up excuses for him and pleading his case.

After nearly three years of dating him throughout college, it was Christmastime. I was going home to be with my family, and my boyfriend was not invited. He was not even welcome in our home. You would think that this would be reason enough for me to dump him, but I was in "love." Looking back, I know that it was really an infatuation, combined with my fear of being alone.

The Lord was really up to something that Christmas. I think it's wonderfully ironic how God chose the time of Jesus' birthday to change my life. I did not like to admit it to myself at the time, but it really bothered me that my family was not accepting of my boyfriend. It weighed heavy on my heart. I looked up to my newly married brother, and had always watched Tate and Ali's relationship with longing stars in my eyes. Marrying into our family, Ali is now as much as a part of my family as any of my siblings are. I wanted that. I know I need that someday. When I came to this realization was when Jesus began strengthening me in ways unimaginable. I wasn't changed overnight, but God had planted a seed in my heart and mind, and I knew I needed for my life to drastically change. On the drive back to Tulsa after Christmas, I prayed and talked to God out loud for hours. He revealed to me that He did have something greater in mind for my life, and that my lack of faith was wounding my relationship with Jesus. He held out His hand for me to hold, and said, "Trust Me."

When I got back to Tulsa, I ended things with my boyfriend. It was the hardest decision I've ever had to make, but God is faithful. I struggled for months with the breakup and almost turned back around, but God refused to let go of my hand and told me to keep moving forward.

Returning from Neverland, I began getting involved in Life Church, I joined a Bible study, and started volunteering for the youth group. I began playing the guitar, doing cross-fit, reading the Bible, and spending more time with Christian women. Like Wendy returning from Neverland to become the woman she was born to be, I came out of my relationship seeking to become the woman God intended for me to be. I am finding my true identity in Christ and discovering my purposes in life. A sense of hope and fulfillment that is all consuming is now present in me, and stretches into all areas of my daily life. I praise God that He changed the conditions of my heart, and pray that He continues to shape and mold me into His image. I know that I will still struggle and sin, but with the power of the Holy Spirit inside of me, through life's challenges, I will choose to remember:

> No test or temptation that comes your way is beyond the course of what others have had to face. All you need to re-member is that God will never let you down; he'll never let

you be pushed past your limit; he'll always be there to help you come through it.

— 1 Corinthians 10:13 (MSG)

When I am faced with a difficult time in life, no matter the circumstance, I will remember God's promise that I can get through any and every trial with the help and guidance of Jesus Christ.

Recently, I found out that one of my old high school friends who was on the cheerleading squad with me is now divorced. She is only twenty-four years old. This makes me so sad for her, but also serves as a realization that every relationship, and even some marriages, do not last. Every serious couple approaches their future with an invincible perspective of being together forever. The truth is, for different reasons, some premarital relationships will fail. While many mismatched dating relationships teach us important lessons about life and may have the potential to be like Northern Stars pointing us in the right direction, some dating relationships just aren't meant to be "till death do us part."

Some people say the healing process takes the same amount of time as the duration of the relationship. You may be fine for a week or a month and then that homesick feeling washes over you and strong emotions flood the heart's shore. Regret, emotional pain, sadness, and defeat creep into your thoughts. *What's wrong with me? Why am I not good enough?* I know that I felt this way initially when I was no longer in a relationship, but the truth of the matter is that you are good enough! I don't want to sound like your mother by saying this, but you are beautiful inside and out. This is something to pray that you will become convicted about personally, but for now, I will tell you the truth; you are unique and special. The Creator of the universe fearfully and wonderfully handcrafted you in His image (Psalm 139:14). Like ketchup, you have something that the world needs. Thank God for His blessing in creating you as you are. Be confident in yourself, and rest assured that you have a God-given purpose in life.

With that, I want to add that while we are called to be strong, confident women of God, we were also born with a need to love, be loved, and nurture the world. God created Eve as a suitable helper for Adam. As women, we naturally want to be that suitable helper to someone special that God had in mind when He created us. I will say that it's okay to be lonely at times and long to be with that "someone special." I know I feel this way at times. This is how we as women were created. But most importantly, never lose sight that your love for God should be placed above all else. He is our one. Jesus Christ wants a personal relationship with each of us. God's love is infinite and never failing. This is because God is love (1 John 4:8). Having a relationship with Jesus is the only way to ever be completely whole, and at peace with who He created you to be. The Lord is able to fill the void in our hearts and lives that no man ever could, but only if we let Him.

It's amazing how God uses pieces of our past to help people who are going through similar struggles. Recently, I got to share my testimony with my women's Bible study group. Later that night, one woman in the group messaged me on Facebook:

> Hey Alex! I just wanted to specifically say thank you for sharing your testimony with the life group! I know it takes courage to be vulnerable and talk about the most difficult

parts of your past, but it meant a lot to me simply knowing that I'm not alone—that others have gone through similar struggles—and it's inspiring hearing how God has helped you overcome certain things and be full of joy today.

I feel incredibly blessed knowing that God used my story to impact somebody's life. I got to witness how God can turn a person's past into their purpose, and then everything made perfect sense. God can use a sinner like me. He can use me to witness to others about Jesus' saving grace. He can use me to help other girls going through similar struggles. He can use me to bring glory to His great name. Today, my heartache is gone. My hurting is finished. I choose to look at my breakup as a blessing and tool that can help others, rather than a burden. I choose to return from Neverland with grace, seeking God wholeheartedly, and finding my true identity in Jesus Christ. The Lord is faithful.

PRAYER:

Dear Jesus, I know that You have a great future in store for me. Show me how to follow Your guiding light in my life. Help me to look for the window of hope that You always provide through difficult circumstances. I pray that I would seek You for direction, love, and contentment. Teach me how to become more like You, and show me how to love others like You have loved me. May all of my endeavors glorify You, Lord. Fill me to the brim, and let Your peace, joy, and wisdom overflow in my life. I need You desperately during this time in my life. Reveal to me Your plans and purposes. Lead me through this, Jesus. It's in Your holy name I pray. Amen.

CHAPTER TWO

LET IT GO!

RECENTLY, I WATCHED THE MOVIE *Frozen*. It was great movie, filled with many lessons for little girls. But what impressed me the most was the soundtrack. The song "Let It Go" really spoke to my heart for some reason because of its message. "Let It Go" is a song about a young princess who has lived in isolation for most of her life because her magical powers, which she cannot control, are dangerous. When the kingdom finds out about her magical powers, she becomes frightened and runs away. The song begins while she is running away.

The snow glows white on the mountain tonight
Not a footprint to be seen
A kingdom of isolation,
And it looks like I'm the queen.

The wind is howling like this swirling storm inside
Couldn't keep it in, heaven knows I tried!

Don't let them in, don't let them see
Be the good girl you always have to be
Conceal, don't feel, don't let them know
Well, now they know!

Let it go, let it go
Can't hold it back anymore
Let it go, let it go
Turn away and slam the door![1]

I love the introduction to this song. It reminds us that we don't have to conceal our hurt. Many girls (myself included) have tried to act like they are A-OK after a devastating breakup. Let me give you a forewarning. This only prolongs the hurt and the emotions that are bound to well up if we don't allow ourselves to experience the feeling of loss. Whether it takes weeks, months, or even years after your breakup, you will need to release your emotions. It's better to let them out now rather than later so that the healing process can begin.

Have you ever watched the movie *The Parent Trap?* Remember when the twins get sent to the "isolation cabin" as punishment for bad behavior? Don't punish yourself by isolation from the world at this time. You were designed with a God-given purpose to glorify God on earth. This requires relation and interaction with people. God created us with a need to be in connection with others. We are relational beings. Neglecting this need can lead to a downward spiral. By this I mean depression, food infatuations, eating disorders, porn, etc. Do not give the Devil a foothold! God Himself said, "It is not good for the man to be alone" (Genesis 2:18).

If a loved one has ever neglected you, you know it is not a pleasant experience. Whether it was your best friend, sister, brother, cousin, or someone else, each of us has experienced being neglected at some point in our lives. While this oversight was most likely not

---

1   Kristen Anderson-Lopez and Rober Lopez, Let It Go. Wonderland Music Company Inc., 2013.

anything personal, it sure felt like it was at the time. The person who you were close to and being neglected by was probably going through something themselves that had nothing to do with you, and the hurt they caused you was not intentional. Still, there was infliction, and scars, left by them in the form of emotional damage. Do not do this to your friends, your little sister, your grandmother, or anyone else you're close to. Just because you are hurting, don't shut out those who love you in return. Based on past experience, I can almost guarantee that the people in your life who love you want to be used as a support system rather than watching you struggle and hurt alone.

> You are the light of the world. A city set on a hill cannot be hidden; nor does anyone light a lamp and put it under a basket, but on the lamp-stand, and it gives light to all who are in the house. Let your light shine before men in such a way that they may see your good works, and glorify your Father who is in heaven.
>
> — Matthew 5:14-16

Don't hide your light. Let it shine! Isolation is not a helpful solution to our problems. People are counting on us to show them and tell them about Christ's unfailing love. "For God, who said, 'Let light shine out of darkness,' made his light shine in our hearts to give us the light of the knowledge of God's glory displayed in the face of Christ" (2 Corinthians 4:6).

I've heard it said that, "Tears are little messengers of the soul that remind us who we are." It is okay to cry. While I don't suggest frequently making a scene, or crying in front of everyone all of the time, speak to your sister, your mom, or your best friend. Let them know exactly what you are going through. Share all of your hurt and pain, because it will make you feel better, and they may have some great advice to offer.

"Let It Go" is symbolic of Princess Elsa laying down her burdens before the world as she and everyone else in the kingdom discover who she really is. This song can be your story too. Let God work through your pain. Become the brave princess He created you to be. Make this breakup a part of your testimony in overcoming the hurt and pain you are going through now, and standing for something greater than you could have ever imagined possible.

Let it go, let it go
And I'll rise like the break of dawn
Let it go, let it go
That perfect girl is gone!

Here I stand
In the light of day
Let the storm rage on,
The cold never bothered me anyway![2]

One of my sorority sisters, Hannah, is a beautiful woman, inside and out. Hannah is a twenty-two-year-old single mother. Her precious little boy's name is Isaiah. The transformation I have witnessed in Hannah after she gave birth to baby Isaiah takes my breath away and brings tears to my eyes every time I think about it. Praise the Lord for His awesome power.

Hannah's testimony is that of faith, courage, and love. After becoming pregnant, keeping the baby was not a choice. It was a

---

2   Kristen Anderson-Lopez and Rober Lopez, Let It Go. Wonderland Music Company Inc., 2013.

conviction of the heart. Hannah would bring the baby into the world, because it was not her decision to make. It was the will of the Lord. During her pregnancy, Hannah started living for Christ. She chose the name Isaiah for her unborn son. The name Isaiah means, "The salvation of the Lord." After I read the story of Isaiah in the Bible over again, I realize now how powerfully fitting the name for Hannah's baby truly is.

The story of Isaiah begins with the wrath of God against His people. The Israelites were living in abundant sin, and unfaithfulness to God. The Lord even refused their offering sacrifices because they were all in vain. The nation would continue to live in sin after their meaningless prayers. God compared the nation of Israel to a prostitute, saying that they kept whoring themselves out to other gods and evil ways. Due to their persistent sin, God claimed to avenge His enemies, and hid His face from Israel. Before God's wrath of punishment fell upon the Israelites, He delivered a message of hope. "I will turn my hand against you; I will thoroughly purge away your dross and remove all your impurities. I will restore your leaders as in days of old, your rulers as at the beginning. Afterward you will be called the City of Righteousness, the Faithful City" (Isaiah 1:25-26). Out of love, The Lord punished Israel, but not before making a promise of deliverance, that He would restore their nation in full, back into the hands of God.

Hannah struggled for a long time during her pregnancy and even for a short duration after Isaiah was born. She struggled with her sense of self-worth, and questioned if God really had a purpose in the plans for her life. *Am I really beautiful?* She wondered. Only when she chose to trust in Jesus, and surrendered her ways to Him in full did she receive a lasting sense of peace, and hope, knowing that the Lord was holding her in His hands and would give her the strength and support she so desperately needed. When Hannah re-dedicated her life to Christ, she was inwardly changed and left with the knowledge of the truth about her worth and beauty. In Psalm 45:11 we read, "Let the king be enthralled by your beauty; honor him, for he is your lord."

Below is a short version of Hannah's testimony. This excerpt was written by Hannah, and briefly explains the Lord's presence in her life through it all. His guiding hand eventually led Hannah to change her mind about her sense of self-worth, and everyone around her witnessed the transformation of her heart.

> I recently read a book called *Do You Think I'm Beautiful?* The main point of the book that really struck a chord in me was when it said, "If the question, 'Do you think I'm beautiful' came attached with every woman's soul, then maybe the question was never meant to come from this world. Maybe the very purpose of the question was to walk me into the presence of my Creator." I've made a lot of bad decisions in my life. I've dealt with feeling unworthy, and inadequate, and wondered if I was really beautiful. But since I stopped living for His love and instead from His love, my life has never been the same. Next week I'm getting baptized along with my entire family. "An outward expression of the inward change."

Is there something that you need to let go of in order to grow closer to the Lord at this time in your life? Lysa Terkeurst talks about letting go in this way: "We aren't in the habit of release. Why? Because of our fear of missing out on some things. But, in the process we miss out on the best things. If we want to discern our Best Yes assignments, we must consider the trade."[3]

For me, it was my ex-boyfriend. After my relationship ended, I began questioning myself, and my decision to be single. My ex and I ended up getting back together several times, but each time we did, things would end, the same as before. Deep down, I knew that although I loved this guy and he was my best friend, it wasn't right. We were not equally yoked and God's hand wasn't the driving force behind our commitment to one another. I knew that God had something else, something greater in mind. That still did not change the fact that ending things with my boyfriend at the time was so incredibly hard. I fought long and hard with God about this one. Eventually God won. He always wins.

God placed people in my life, and put me in situations that enabled me to see my relationship for what it really was. Through prayer and petition, God gave me a resounding peace about my decision. Since the breakup, my identity has become that of Christ. He is now on the throne of my heart and is the King of my life.

Sometimes I miss things about that relationship (the companionship part especially) but I am such a more joyful person now than ever before. My friends and family have even told me that it is obvious that I am a much happier person; and I know personally that I am way more content. There is joy in my heart and my soul is at rest.

---

3   Lysa Terkeurst, *The Best Yes Study Guide: Making Wise Decisions in the Midst of Endless Demands*. https://books.google.nl/books?id=n_W0AwAAQBAJ&pg=PT99&lpg=PT 99&dq=lysa+terkeurst+we+aren%27t+in+the+habit+of+release&source=bl&ots=tr BUrD3Ylf&sig=M3jP5KzG9rHeIyYg4iA-k_yn-9g&hl=en&sa=X&ei=rCdTVe7hN 8r9UIufgbgN&ved=0CCIQ6AEwAA#v=onepage&q=lysa%20terkeurst%20we%20 aren't%20in%20the%20habit%20of%20release&f=false. Accessed May 20, 2015.

Closing the door to a relationship, and daring to enter a new season in life is easier said than done. Oftentimes "love is blind" in the sense that when we are in love (or think we are at least), it is hard to see things for what they really are. I was in an unhealthy relationship, but refused to acknowledge this fact because of my emotional ties to my ex-boyfriend. It is always a wise idea to listen to friends and family's opinions about a significant other. Whether or not you choose to act on their advice is completely up to you, but at least listen to it, and give it time to digest.

Listen to advice and accept instruction, and in the end you will be wise.

— Proverbs 19:20

Choosing to break up once and for all was the hardest decision I've ever had to make; but when I chose to let it go, and surrendered my life to God in full, I was set free. It's been one of the best decisions of my life. I will continue to battle my insecurities with Scripture and biblical wisdom, knowing that God's power has already been made perfect through my weakness (2 Corinthians 12:9). Jesus has my heart completely. I will continue to use my testimony for the rest of my life as a double-edged sword, realizing what God has already done in me, and bringing certain death upon Satan's spiritual attacks.

Regardless of how strong or brave you may be, there will be tough times. On the days where all you want to do is lay in bed and cry, remember the verse Philippians 4:13: "For I can do all things through Christ who strengthens me." Philippians 4:13 is a powerful, yet underrated verse. Although many Christians have memorized this verse, oftentimes it is recited with no zeal, as if it holds no true meaning. I've empowered this verse by replacing the personal pronouns with my name, and encourage you to do the same. "For *Alexandra* can do *all* things through Christ who strengthens her." When writing, I am careful to not make definite bold statements, using the words always or all, unless what I am saying is entirely true. This verse says that we can do *all* things through Christ. This word alone makes this verse a bold statement. In Philippians 4:13, the word *all* empowers the gospel and proves that the passion of Christ is real. Jesus died the most horrible death on a cross to take away our sins, so that we may be forgiven and have eternal life. His death was not in vain. Without sin, Jesus was the perfect sacrifice. God loves you so much that He gave up His only son so that if you believe in Him, you will not perish but have everlasting life (John 3:16). Jesus is alive today. If you believe this is the truth, and want Jesus to be the King and ruler of your life, accept the Lord's invitation and ask Jesus into your heart. Even if Jesus is already your personal Lord and Savior, it is good to be reminded of your conviction.

PRAY THIS PRAYER OUT LOUD:

> Jesus, I come before You now to profess that I am a sinner in need of a Savior. I believe in my heart that You lived a perfect life, died on the cross to take away my sins, and rose from the dead three days later. I know that You are the Almighty God. I want Your Holy Spirit to live inside of me, so that I may live for you and have eternal life in heaven someday. Come into my heart. Come into my life. Forgive me of my past sins and make me a new creation. I love you, Jesus. It's in Your holy, precious name I pray. Amen.

CHAPTER THREE

'TIS THE SEASON

IT WAS MY TWENTY-THIRD BIRTHDAY. I still remember it like it was yesterday. I was sitting across from the person I considered my best friend at the time, having lunch. Recently, Sara had gotten a boyfriend, and recently I had broken up with my boyfriend of three years. I was portraying singleness in a positive light, telling her about the endless possibilities of this season of my life when she made a comment to me that came out of left field. "Maybe it's just not your time yet, Alex," she said. I was shocked. Her comment really rubbed me the wrong way and was hurtful; but at the same time, I realized how wrong she was! I replied, "You know what, you're wrong. I'm young, single, beautiful, and loving life! It is my time."

Singleness is a blessing from God. It is a time to discover your purpose in life and find peace and contentedness in your present circumstances. It is a time for spiritual growth, productivity, and the establishment of oneself. Singleness is not a time to sulk, accomplish nothing, or to be unhappy with your current season of life. If you choose to have a negative attitude about being single now, you run the risk of being unhappy in the next chapter of your life, and the next one after that, and the next one, and the next! Once you are married, having a husband will not be enough. Once you have children, you will wish you had more free time. When your kids become teenagers, you will be eager for them to go off to college and be independent. After your children get married, you will desperately want grandbabies . . . The list could go on and on. I encourage you to start practicing being happy in the current season of your life. Enjoy every moment now, and make it a habit of living a joyful, prayer-filled life of thanksgiving. Count your blessings. Instead of always dwelling on the negative, what you don't have, thank God for everything He has given you. When a negative thought forms in your mind, before you start feeling sorry for yourself, thank your heavenly Father for something great He has done in your life. Someday you will look back and wish that you had taken advantage of more opportunities in life, or you will be content in knowing that you lived life to the fullest.

An admirable young woman I know, whose love for Jesus radiates from her spirit, views being single in this way

> I'm only nineteen almost twenty. I don't have life all figured out. I don't have everything together. I'm still growing into the person God has made me to be. And although most people don't like the "preparation season" or the "growing season" of life, it's actually a very beautiful thing. There are still lots of things I need to work on and areas God needs to strengthen me in. I'd much rather enjoy this season of life growing as a better person, and becoming stronger in areas where I am weak, so that I can be a better daughter, a better friend, and a better wife and mother someday. Most people don't like being single and think it's the worst. Being single does have its not-so-happy times, but it is a beautiful,

beautiful thing. It's time where we can be a better person and grow. We always can be growing and learning to be a better person. Nobody is perfect and we will never be until the day we are called home. I'm so excited for this season of growth. Life is a beautiful thing if you look at it with the right perspective. —Taylor

Like a flower, an aging soul can either blossom or wither away. When we grow old and our hair turns grey, we may not be considered pretty by the world's standards, but our spirits can be beautiful. If we are striving to become more like Christ and diligently striving after His own heart, we are all the more beautiful regardless of our age. Our external beauty can fade quickly, but we can become more holy and righteous by living for God, and by focusing on what is true, noble, right, pure, and lovely (Philippians 4:8). By focusing on these things, our spirit can be uplifted, and we can exude Jesus' light to others; but if our thoughts are only selfish, and focused on the things of this world, our joyful spirit quickly changes into a negative attitude and outlook on life. This kind of selfish thinking leads to selfish living. Let us set our thoughts on heavenly things, so that we may blossom and bring love, joy, and peace to others. May we continue to cultivate and nurture our souls, allowing our inner, true beauty to bloom. Colossians 3:2 says, "Set your minds on things above, not on earthly things."

By being thankful through all situations, God gives us lasting joy despite our circumstances. My friend, Chelsea, accepted a spiritual challenge called "100 Days of Thankfulness." For one hundred days, Chelsea chose to think of, and take note of, different ways God had blessed her. Chelsea used this challenge to witness to others and wrote a post, including a picture of each daily blessing on Facebook. She did this for one hundred days consistently. Not only did this change Chelsea's life perspective, but also, it influenced others by spurring them on to consider areas in their lives where God had blessed them. Whether it is a character trait, a great singing voice, a wonderful family, the ability to cook, a financial situation, or a relative's change of heart, the Lord has granted you blessings in so many ways. Recognize these gifts, have a joyful heart, and maintain a spirit of thanksgiving, so that others may be impacted by your zeal for life.

Rejoice always, pray continually, give thanks in all circumstances; for this is God's will for you in Christ Jesus.

— 1 Thessalonians 5:16-18

Christ wants to make us beautiful to Him by being thankful for our blessings, and loving others. The free gift of salvation is the greatest blessing of all. Because of Jesus' ultimate sacrifice, dying on the cross to take away our sins, we are forgiven and free.

The Priceless Clock

Time is free,
But it's priceless.
You can't own it,
But you can use it.
You can't keep it,
But you can spend it.
Once you've lost it,
You can never get it back.
(Anonymous)

Look carefully then how you walk, not as unwise, but as wise, making the best use of the time, because the days are evil. Therefore do not be foolish, but understand what the will of the Lord is.
— Ephesians 5:15-17

You may realize that now you have a lot more time on your hands. Less companionship can be one of the most difficult aspects of coming out of a relationship. Still, God calls us to be faithful even in the little things (Luke 16:10). This applies to how we spend our time.

Spend your time faithfully striving to be more like Christ. Jesus was single His entire life, and He lived life to the fullest. Jesus spent most of His time on earth loving and caring for people. He had a group of close companions, the disciples, and He taught everyone He came into contact with about God's love either through His words or actions.

The present day and age is far different than when Jesus lived on the Earth. You might be asking yourself, *How can I live my life as a daughter of Christ right now?* Play an instrument, adopt a pet, journal, sponsor a child, talk to an older Christian woman, send encouraging notes, memorize Bible verses, ride a bike, train for a half marathon, call your grandmother, find your volunteering niche, or meet people— simply try something new! Let everything you do bring glory to God. There's so many different ways to have fun and take your mind off of things. This list contains many recommendations of how to maintain a productive, Christian lifestyle. These activities are ones that have worked for me, making me a happier, more positive person in my time of singleness. I hope that this list will help motivate and empower you too, as you strive to live life to the fullest during this precious season.

1. **Seek a godly perspective from an older Christian woman** (Hebrews 10:24-25). She doesn't have to be much older than you. Just a few years. Kelly, the girl who disciples me, is only three years older than I am. As sisters in Christ, we are called to encourage one another in our walk of faith.

2. **Meet new people** (1 Corinthians 15:33). Get out of your house! Be outgoing and friendly. Form friendships with your friend's

friends. Join a women's club, college or sorority alumni group, take cooking classes, join the church choir, join a gym, meet your neighbors, help the little old lady next door—it doesn't matter! Do anything and everything to get out and about and be around people. In saying this, be careful about spending too much time with people you know that are bad influences to your Christian morals. You are at a vulnerable time in your life right now. It is wise to choose spiritually strengthening companions.

3. **Join a small group** (Colossians 3:16). Joining a women's Bible study and a singles life group through Life Church was the best thing I did right after college. These people soon became my friends—my real friends, my best friends. We do fun things together like play sand volleyball, go out dancing on the weekends, watch movies, and celebrate birthday parties. They are such a blessing in my life, and I don't know how I would have gotten over my past relationship without these people constantly building me up. God commands us to encourage each other in Christ, teaching and sharing the wisdom of the Bible with one another.

4. **Become a part of an outdoor sports league.** Tennis, sand volleyball, kickball, softball, soccer—there are so many different teams to choose from. During the summer, I play tennis weekly. I bring the jam box, tennis racquet, and my A game, and my partner and I go play. It's great exercise and a lot of fun! Ask around or look up online how to become a part of one of these co-ed recreational sports leagues.

5. **Volunteer** (1 Timothy 6:18). Volunteering may seem daunting and intimidating at first, but once you find your volunteer niche, God will bless you for your heart of service and compassion. When helping others, you are putting God's love on display for the world to see. Not only will volunteering leave you with a lasting sense of peace and joy, but also you are storing up for yourself treasures in heaven.

6. **Pick up an instrument** (Psalm 95:1, Colossians 3:16, Ephesians 5:19). I recently started playing the guitar. I found a cheap Jasmine Acoustic on Amazon.com and ordered it. There are so many great tutorials on YouTube to get started. UltimateGuitar.com is a great resource to show you the chords to play a wide variety of genres, including Christian praise and worship songs. Any

kind of musical instrument is sweet medicine to the soul. The Bible mentions music in many different contexts in the Bible. Let your music be glorifying to God!

7. Make a blog (Ephesians 4:29). Writing is a great way to express oneself. Since blogs are open to the public, they should not be used as a diary, but can speak encouraging words of grace to an audience.

8. Send encouraging notes (Proverbs 12:25). Kelly, the woman who disciples me, has a heart for helping and encouraging other people. She finds joy in writing simple, spiritually uplifting notes to others. In doing this, she demonstrates Christ's love.

9. Sponsor a child. I used to sponsor an inner city kid to go to Kids Across America, a Christian sports camp, each year. It never failed that I was emotionally moved when I received a thank-you letter in return from one of the campers who was able to go to camp, have fun, and learn about the love of Jesus Christ. Now, my vision has expanded and my outreach has become more global. If you are looking to sponsor a child in another country, World Vision is a trusted Christian organization that sponsors children in the areas where help is most needed. This organization really connects you to the child you are sponsoring through exchanging letters, pictures, and e-mails throughout the year. The little girl's name that I sponsor is Dorass. She is five years old and is from Malawi, Africa.

10. Adopt a pet. I thought long and hard about getting a dog. I ended up getting a guitar instead, but I still want a dog to this day! According to WebMD, animals can improve people's mood in terms of depression and wellbeing. Cats and dogs offer companionship, social interaction, touch, activity, responsibility, and "uncomplicated love." A pet will love you no matter what! I've heard that there are even some pet-adoption organizations that need people to foster homeless pets while they search for a permanent owner. While there is no biblical teaching I know of that supports getting a pet, in Genesis Adam was ordained by God as the caretaker of all of the animals in the garden of Eden.

11. Learn how to cook. Nobody said you have to be a Mozart of a chef, but at least try! Cooking and baking can be fun; and who knows, you might become really good at it! Turn on a fun play list in the kitchen and rock out in your adorable apron! I am no Rachael Ray, but I enjoy baking simple sweets every once in a while. Here is a melt-in-your-mouth dessert recipe I like to call, "Crazy Brownies." This recipe is simple, but leaves everyone sugar crazed and smiling.

CRAZY BROWNIES

What you will need:

- Brownie mix (which usually requires one egg and vegetable oil)
- Break-apart chocolate chip cookie dough (12-count package)
- 12 Reese's Peanut Butter Cups
- Muffin pan
- Non-stick baking spray

Spray the muffin pan with plenty of non-stick baking spray. Combine the ingredients together for the brownie mix in a separate bowl. Place one cookie dough square in each section of the muffin pan. Put a Reese's Peanut Butter Cup on top of each piece of cookie dough. Smother each cook dough piece and Reese's with brownie mix. Bake at 350 degrees for 12-20 minutes.

12. Spend Time with Family. My great-grandmother is ninety-four years old. Joannie lives in a house by herself and still drives! I know that I am very blessed to have her in my life. I also know that when I come over to Joannie's house and spend time with her playing a game of Rummikub, or just telling her what's new in my life, her day becomes so much brighter. (She has told me this.) Not only do I enjoy hanging out with her, but also she gives great advice! Ninety-four-year-old women of God are wise by nature. It gives me joy in making her life, which must seem despondent at times, a little more cheerful. But, in all actuality, I am on the receiving end in our relationship. I am so grateful that God put this sweet little old lady in my life to serve as a beacon of light! Being able to spend time with her is such a blessing.

13. Ride a bike (1 Corinthians 3:16-17). Riding my bike brings me back to my childhood. Recently, I met a girl on an airplane from Austin, Texas, who sold her car and was relying on a bike as her sole means of transportation. While this is not exactly what I am recommending, it is important to maintain a healthy lifestyle.

14. Train for a 10K (Proverbs 27:17). Every year, I run the Ft. Worth Turkey Trot with my little sister, Alison. This year, we decided to run the 10K. I trained for this 6.2-mile race in Tulsa, and Alison trained in Texas. Even though I did not get to train with my sister, I did not train alone. I knew that I wouldn't and simply couldn't motivate myself if I tried to prepare for that long Turkey run with no one there to push me. I paired up with one of my friends, Emily, who was training for a half marathon at the time. The 6.21371 mile race was the longest distance I've ever run, but on the day of the race, I ran it in 55 minutes! It was a major accomplishment. Afterwards, I felt free to eat whatever I wanted that Thanksgiving Day!

I did not run alone because I did not want to risk not training my hardest or pushing myself. I ran with another person for motivation. In the same way, God calls us as Christians to build each other up and push each other to strive to do our best in living for Christ. Hopefully someday soon, I will train for and run a half marathon with my little sister.

15. Memorize verses (1 Timothy 4:13). I am good at remembering words and numbers. This is helpful for me to be able to memorize Scripture. But even if you are not good at strict memorization, by remembering the messages of verses, God's Word can be ingrained on our hearts. Memorizing Scripture is a joyful experience that leaves me with a sense of joy and fulfillment.

16. Pray for you future spouse (Proverbs 18:22, 1 Corinthians 6:18). Pray that your future husband would be preparing himself for marriage and making the most of this time during his singleness. Pray that you would both trust God's perfect timing for meeting one another—being patient, and faithfully waiting. There is no better time than now to learn how to be faithful to your spouse. As you pursue purity, pray that God would guide and protect you and your future husband, teaching you both to flee from sexual immorality, by guarding your hearts and minds in Christ Jesus.

17. **Photography, scrapbooking, drawing, writing a journal, taking a road trip, starting a small business, or** _____
. . . the possibilities are limitless. I believe that finding a hobby that you are passionate about is really important. You might not be passionate about the hobby you choose to pursue initially, but through perseverance, passion could develop. Stick with it, and you might actually find an activity that makes your heart hum with happiness. What is your soul calling you to do right now that you have not prioritized yet? Write your own hobby, task, or goal that you wish to accomplish in the blank. If you can't think of anything specific, pray that God would lead you in that direction. Listen to His voice, and He will reveal to you something that is unique, special, and specifically important for you to carry out.

CHAZOWN

One way to prioritize Jesus Christ as the most important part of your life is by spending your time in a way that is glorifying to the Father. In finding out who we are as daughters of Christ, we must take intentional steps of action that will lead us to the cross. Allow Him to work in your life to find out who you are and discover your God-given purpose in life by giving your life to Christ and living life chasing after God's own heart.

When I was younger, I did a Bible study that was focused on developing a purpose-driven life. In one part of the study, I wrote a bulleted list:

BENEFITS OF A PURPOSE-DRIVEN LIFE

- Knowing your purpose will give your life meaning.
- By discovering your purpose, your life will become simpler.
- After knowing your purpose, your life will become more focused.
- Knowing your purpose will make your life better.
- By knowing your purpose you are prepared for eternity.

We each have a divine purpose and gifts that have been specifically assigned to us from God. Our passions, hobbies, hopes, and dreams are good indicators that can point us in the right direction to discover our God-given purpose in life. Without purpose, life has no meaning. In finding our purpose, we are better able to use our gifts and talents to bring glory to God.

Recently, I did a workshop through LifeChurch.tv called "Chazown." Chazown is a Hebrew word that means dream, revelation, or vision. God has a dream for each of our lives. By combining my past experiences (good and bad), core values, and spiritual gifts, I was able to define a Chazown for my life.

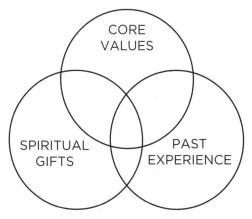

God created me with a dream for my life: To use the resources and spiritual gifts God has blessed me with to further His kingdom.

- *To be a Christian author* - to encourage people, to evangelize, and to witness to others through writing about my past experiences.
- *To be a teacher* - to impact students' lives through my actions, and through valuable lessons about life.

- *To be a godly leader* - to impact others through my everyday life. God wants to use my words and deeds to spread the good news about Christ's love.
- *To be a Christian philanthropist* - to use the money God blesses me with to further His kingdom.

What is God's vision for your life? What is your Chazown?

PRESENCE

"Martha, Martha," The Lord answered, "you are worried and upset about many things, but few things are needed—or indeed, only one. Mary has chosen what is better, and it will not be taken away from her."

— Luke 10:41-42

At Christmastime, life becomes overwhelmingly chaotic. Unfortunately, sometimes the true celebration of Christmas, Christ's birth, gets overlooked. In the same way, our lives can become so crazy that we forget what this life is all about. While serving the Lord does please God, we should not spend so much time being concerned with worldly affairs and helping others that our time spent with Him is actually compromised. There is even an extent to which doing acts of service can inhibit our own personal spiritual growth.

Being a Christian missionary is like a Brita pitcher. We pour out purified water to others in the form of the gospel and by demonstrating Christ's love. The most annoying part of a Brita pitcher is changing the filter. In order for the water to be clean and produce the purest water possible, the filter must be changed frequently. In the same way, we must spiritually rejuvenate ourselves through the

Word, in prayer, and by listening to godly wisdom. What was once used to help and hydrate others has the ability to become murky and unhealthy if we do not take care of our own spiritual needs first.

Like Martha, Jesus wants us to come, sit at His feet, and listen to what He has to say. He wants us to simply come and be in His presence. When I spend time with family or friends, I make it a point to offer my presence. What I mean by this is that I try to be there mentally, as well as physically, paying attention to what people are saying, verbal or nonverbal, and really connecting with whomever I am with. Spending time in the Word and in prayer is how we connect with God and offer Him our presence. Offering my presence does not always depend on the length of time I spend with someone. "It's not the quantity of time, but the quality." The same is true when it comes to spending time with the Lord. I try not to place parameters on my time spent in the presence of God, because my relationship with Jesus is not dependent on the amount of time I spend with Him each and every day. Rather than going through the motions, my relationship with Christ is dependent on my humbling myself in God's presence, and sincerely devoting my time to Him through the Word and in prayer.

FOR SUCH A TIME AS THIS

Esther was taken as a wife for King Ahasuerus, the king of the Medes and Persians, despite being a Jew. Living in the kingdom, Esther learned that Haman, an evil man, was plotting to kill all of the Jews of the land. Esther confronted her uncle, Mordecai, and sought his advice as to what to do. Mordecai's advice came with a requirement: great faith. His advice to Esther was that she needed to confront the king. Although Esther served as a wife to King Ahasuerus, she was not the technical queen.

She was not royalty; therefore, by law she needed to have a personal request from the king in order to pay him a visit. Without this request she ran the risk of being killed. Mordecai encouraged Esther to do the right thing and told her that she might have been divinely chosen to be Ahasuerus' wife, "For such a time as this" (Esther 4:14). Despite her fears, Esther responded in faith. She confronted King Ahasuerus. Haman's wicked plans were then revealed, and her people were saved.

Esther trusted God, and because of her faith and obedience, the Lord was able to do great things through her. The same can be true with our lives. God's power and authority is limitless, and He can use us to do great things.

Prayer fuels our faith. I bet that Esther spent many hours on her knees in prayer before she confronted the king. The power of prayer is greater than any concept or perception we could ever grasp.

PRAYER:

Jesus, I strive after many things. Let my number one pursuit be You. I pray that I would rise to the occasion of Your calling and the purposes You have for my life. Give me the courage to follow You wholeheartedly, Jesus. Enable me with strength and wisdom to spread Your name to the ends of the earth. Help me to accept and rejoice in Your role for my life. Let me recognize the beauty and grace in the plans You have specifically assigned for me. For such a time as this, give me strength to be bold in my faith and stand up for what I believe in. Amen.

CHAPTER FOUR

CUBIC ZIRCONIA VS. DIAMOND

DIAMONDS ARE MADE OF CARBON that has been crystallized over the duration of millions of years. These rare gems are formed deep within the earth's crust—about 150 kilometers deep. Intense heat, crushing, and pressure are applied during the formation process. Diamonds may be found near the surface of earth's crust through a geological process where magma forces its way up through the crust and explosively erupts at the surface. When this magma sweeps through a diamond-rich area, only then are diamonds relocated to a reachable distance from the earth's surface.

The diamond is a beautiful gem that holds much value. This is why real diamonds are made into expensive pieces of jewelry and sold in the form of precious earrings, bracelets, necklaces, and rings. The diamond in the form of a wedding ring holds special meaning due to its rarity. Cubic zirconia, on the other hand, sparkles brighter than a diamond and exudes brilliant colors. So why don't people just use CZs for wedding rings? This is because they are not precious gems, and therefore hold little value. The CZ is not a real diamond. It's a fake! God wants to mold us into beautiful diamonds. Living sold-out lives for Christ is the only way to become like a diamond. A diamond's worth is far more in the eyes of the Lord than a CZ. Be the diamond He created you to be. God is for you, so who can be against you (Romans 8:31)!

My favorite fairytale is Cinderella. I think that we can all learn a lot from Cinderella's character. Before her mother died at a young age, she taught Ella to be kind and have courage in all things. As she grows up, Ella becomes a lovely maiden who does not have a mean bone in her body. The kindness she possesses is unconditional and her zeal for life is captivating. When Cinderella's father dies, her stepmother and two stepsisters take advantage of Cinderella's beautiful spirit. They boss her around, make fun of her, force her to cook and clean up after them, and shun her to live by herself in the attic. Still, abundant joy overflows from the depths of her soul, and she sings with joy in her heart day after day. Her situation looks despondent, but God always provides an open window when all of the doors are shut. The upcoming ball was Cinderella's open window. After her stepmother forbids her to go, magical forces come to rescue Cinderella and usher her to the ball. Cinderella shines like a diamond in the rough at the ball where she attracts her prince charming. When the midnight bell strikes, Cinderella abruptly disappears but leaves behind one of her glass slippers. When the prince goes in search of Cinderella, and shows up at her house, Cinderella's stepmother locks her in the attic. Good always triumphs evil. After much adversity, prince charming finds Cinderella, the glass slipper fits, and the two live happily ever after.

That's all we really want, right? *A happily ever after.* This longing is ingrained in our DNA. It's part of who we are as women, daughters of Eve, and as human beings. Most women want to be swept off of their feet, to find and marry a prince charming. The problem is that we oftentimes grow impatient—impatient of enduring the cooking and cleaning, the isolation, and the hardship. We interfere with God's timing. We sell ourselves short to the wrong prince charming or to other things that we hope will fill us. We develop bad habits caused by anxiety and lack of self-worth. We stop having faith in our God who has a plan. Despite all of our doubting, God's grace remains upon us, and His plans prevail. The Cinderella story reminds me of how God's plans always unfold the way He intends, despite any manipulation or obstacles that I may try to place in the way.

At one point during the time after my serious relationship ended, I let fear creep in. I had just moved into a new rental house by myself and was living alone until I could find a girl to live with me. It was only two months after the breakup. The house was beautiful. People said that I would love living there. It was the summer, and although I had a part-time job working at a women's shoe store boutique, I still had lots of free time. The next three months of my life, before Katie moved in, was the loneliest time I had yet experienced. Not having that companionship in the form of a significant other, on top of being by myself in a new house, really took a toll on me in those months. The emptiness of that house constantly reminded me of the newfound void in my life.

Right after the breakup, I refused to let God in, and my life was rough because of it. I became so afraid of not being loved (by someone other than my dad and mom) that I set up props that were based around my fears. I became involved in online dating and began striving to find someone, just for comfort's sake. I did end up going on a few dates, and even met a Christian guy who was a really nice person and who had strong morals and treated me right. But God did not choose to bless that relationship. It wasn't online dating that was the problem, but rather the conditions of my heart.

Relearning how to live my life started with baby steps. It wasn't until I began meeting with Kelly, the woman who disciples me, that my perspective on being single began to change. Having Christian accountability encouraged me to stay strong. "Be strong in the Lord in the strength of his might" (Ephesians 6:10). Our talks reminded me that my value is not based on the conditions of my life, but rather the conditions of my heart; and my self-worth is found in my identity in Christ.

For I can do all things through Christ who strengthens me.
— Philippians 4:13

Walk through your fears. Every time you set a prop in place or let fear creep in, it's like pouring gasoline on a fire! Don't feed your fears, but rather, walk through them. Remove the props of anxiety, worry, lack of self-worth, and fear. Live life with confident faith in God's plans. As you learn to put your trust in God more than in your fears, they will loosen their grip on your life, and your relationship with Christ will be fortified because of your faith.

Although there are many girls out there like me, not every girl struggles with the fear of being alone. You might be thinking, *So how can I apply this advice to my life?* Everyone is afraid of something. Some people claim they're not, but this is only a mask of pride. Below is an activity that will help you identify your personal fear, show you ways that your fear is flawed (because it is a lie from the Devil), and demonstrate how to surrender your fear to God.

1. Identify your fear that inhibits you from putting your full trust in the Lord. Example: *Being alone for the rest of my life.*

2. On a scale of 1-10, how likely is this fear? 3

3. On a scale of 1-10, how unlikely is this fear? 9

4. Consider if the two Richter scales even add up to ten! Now, take time to realize that the *unlikely* scale is more accurate than the likely.

5. Why do you think you have this fear? Journal about it, or list your thoughts on this question.

6. Present your request to God. Prayer is a mighty weapon to fight Satan's spiritual attacks. Ask God to take away your fear and strengthen you in this area of your life.

Lord God, I have been struggling with the fear of being alone. I pray, God, that You would take this fear away from me. Help me to remember that this fear is a lie from the Devil. I trust You, Lord. You work in ways that I cannot see, but give me faith that I might believe. For it is the kind of faith that moves mountains that I want to uphold. Give me the wisdom to discern that this lie, in the form of fear, is not the truth. In the Bible it says that Your plans are to prosper and not to harm me, plans to give me a hope and a future (Jeremiah 29:11). Help me remember this always, and when anxiety washes over me God, by prayer and petition I will surrender my fear to You, Lord, and Your peace, which transcends all understanding will guard my heart and mind in Christ Jesus (Philippians 4:6-7). I yearn for this kind of peace and rest, which can only be found in You, Lord. Help me to continuously seek Your face and walk in Your ways. I love you, Jesus. It's in Your mighty name I pray. Amen.

7. Flush it! Using your least favorite color of marker, write your fear on a piece of toilet paper, and send it directly to where it belongs.

Nobody can protect you from the emotional damage a breakup causes, except Christ. Choosing to move forward and become a living testimony to other girls who are going through a similar trial or temptation enabled me to be more concerned for others, taking the focus off of myself. In the name of Jesus, and for the sake of what God has taught you through your struggle, act as a Christian leader for younger girls and women of all ages by applying sound advice from the Bible to your life and demonstrating Christ's love. Your testimony is a powerful tool that has the ability to shape a diamond. Be the diamond God created you to be. Become a living message of hope to other women, a symbol of God's power and love.

CHAPTER FIVE

BEAUTIFUL THINGS

WHEN I READ THE BOOK of Hosea (Hosea 1-14) at thirteen years old, I remember being puzzled, asking myself, *Why would God punish a holy man by telling him to marry a prostitute?*

The story of Gomer and Hosea begins when God asks Hosea to marry a prostitute. Obedient to God's will, Hosea takes Gomer as his wife. The couple begins having children, and God commands Hosea to name his three children these names that have been translated from Hebrew to their English meanings: "Jezreel" (foreshadowing the punishment of Israel), "Lo-Ruhamah" (no mercy), and "Lo-Ammi" (not my people). These names were all in correlation to the unfaithful nation of Israel at the time. Gomer ran away from her husband to other men on several accounts. On one such occasion, Gomer was sold into slavery by one of her lovers. Each time, Hosea retrieved his wife in a kind and gentle manner. He even bought her out of slavery to come back home. Hosea demonstrated unconditional love towards his wife, Gomer.

What I didn't realize at thirteen years old was that the book of Hosea is not a story just about Gomer and Hosea. This story is truly about Israel, and is a beautiful precedent of God's enduring love. The nation of Israel had become so distant from God, yet the Lord never forsakes them. Ultimately, Israel received punishment in the form of captivity. Yet, our God is a compassionate God, and He always welcomes back His people with open arms. The book of Hosea ends with a plea that Israel return to the Lord, and a promise that He will restore their nation in full. God used the story of Hosea and Gomer to be an example of God's relentless love and mercy toward Israel, His chosen people.

The Lord may want to use your story to witness to other women about the essence of God's infinite love and mercy. No matter how far you have gone astray, God wants you back in His arms. According to the book of Hosea, the Lord yearns for you to fully surrender your life and your ways to Him. Commit yourself to an eternal relationship with Jesus Christ, and experience love in its fullest form.

Virginity and purity are two separate entities. While virginity can be lost, purity is a state of being. Purity represents spiritual wellness, our relationship with Christ. "The Lord does not look at the things people look at. People look at the outward appearance, but the Lord looks at the heart" (1 Samuel 16:7). God is constantly refining me. He is always at work in my heart and in my life, molding me like a potter molds clay. By Christ's love and mercy, through the forgiveness of my sins, I can be purified spiritually and emotionally. "For it is by grace you have been saved through faith—and this is not from yourselves, it is the gift of God—not by works, so that no one can boast"

(Ephesians 2:8-9). Regardless of our past, through Jesus' redeeming love and grace, we can become pure again. Because of the cross, we are forgiven and free.

When Christ looks at me, He does not see all of my past sins; instead He looks on me with love and compassion. Our God is the Lord of the present, which means that He does not hold our sins against us. I think God coined the term "forgive and forget." He does not dwell on the sins of our past, but instead He cares about the current state of our spiritual wellbeing. The Bible gives us this promise: "If we confess our sins, he is faithful and just and will forgive us our sins and purify us from all unrighteousness" (1 John 1:9). This does not give us a fast pass to sin. Quite the opposite. It is a call to action. It means that we are held to a higher standard: to be obedient followers of Jesus Christ this very day, this very moment.

As Christians we are called to be the light of the world, and set the precedent of demonstrating Jesus' love and forgiveness. We are to forgive and forget just as Christ does the same for us each and every day. The Bible issues us this warning, "For if you forgive men when they sin against you, your heavenly Father will also forgive you. But if you do not forgive men their sins, your Father will not forgive your sins" (Matthew 6:14-15).

There is an interesting pattern throughout the Bible, where God chooses to use the people who are broken in spirit and in lowly positions of prestige on earth to carry out His message. David, the youngest of his brothers, was a shepherd boy. In biblical times, the throne naturally went to the eldest, or the second born if the first was ineligible, and so on. God anointed David as king despite the fact that he was the youngest of the eight brothers. If we look back at the election, David wasn't even considered in the lottery when the elders were choosing who should be king out of all of Jesse's sons. Yet, it was God's will for David to be king. The Bible says that David had a heart after God's own heart. When the elders refused the first seven sons, they asked one final time if any other brothers remained. Jesse was probably in a bewildered state of shock when he responded, "There remains yet the youngest, and there he is keeping the sheep." And Samuel said to Jesse, "Send and bring him. For we will not sit down till he comes here" (1 Samuel 16:11). Samuel and the elders did not even sit down until David had arrived! It makes me wonder how far away David actually was. Did it take hours, or even days before he arrived? When David entered the house of his father, Samuel heard the Lord say, "Arise, anoint him; for this *is* the one" (v. 12)!

Ruth, a lowly widow, found favor in the eyes of the Lord and married Boaz, a man of God, against all odds. These two were actually David's great grandparents, and part of the lineage of Christ. This shows that the Lord works in wonderful and mysterious ways. He chooses to do great works through people who seek His face. We don't always know His plans, and we sometimes don't even find out the results of our acts of obedience until we get to heaven. Even so, we are called to be obedient and carry out the will of God. David didn't know that one day he would become a great ruler. Still, he remained faithful, and was found righteous in the Lord's eyes. Ruth didn't know that one of her grandbabies would become the divinely selected king over Israel, or that she would be part of the procession of the lineage of Christ. She was simply being faithful in taking care of her mother-in-law, Naomi, when great things began to happen. By remaining faithful in the little things, God blessed Ruth immensely.

We influence the people around us more than we think. We influence the way they look at Christianity and their perspective of Jesus based on the way they see us live our lives, and the words they hear us speak. As Christians, we are called to walk by faith and not by sight. Our role is simply to live our lives as seed-planters, embedding the gospel into other people's lives. We may never even see what becomes of those seeds, but God calls us to remain faithful in the act of what I like to call "seed planting."

Seed planting is a broad term for spreading God's Word, and sharing the gospel. Sometimes the seed of the gospel that we plant into people's hearts and lives will not flourish or grow immediately. In fact, it may not grow at all. Yet, even if one seed planted does not thrive, other seeds will. Christ's love is unconditional. In the same way, we should demonstrate Jesus' grace and love toward others despite any definite, visible, or tangible guarantees or rewards.

God produces good fruit that keeps multiplying. Seed planting is what we are called to do according to the Bible. I am not perfect. There are many ways I would like to strengthen my relationship with Christ, but despite my imperfection, I am called to go and make disciples of all the nations (Matthew 28:19).

I used to think evangelism was something that I was not good at. As my love for God grew, this thought really bothered me, so I decided to do something about it. I took a free evangelism course online, Evangelism 101, that taught me how to better share my faith.

The most important thing I took away from the course was not the memorized passages, or eloquent ways to tell the story of Jesus Christ. This story, written by Dr. Ludwig Van Otto, gives a beautiful illustration of what I learned:

> I have met some wonderful Christians in my eighty-plus years. One of my favorites is a paralyzed (from her neck to her toes) black woman I met in 1975. I was pastor of a small church, going to seminary, and working a part-time job to support my family. She lived in a poor part of south Fort Worth in a very old house. When I entered her home, she was laying on a chair made into a bed. She could not sit. She could only lie flat on this "homemade" bed, but she was friendly and talked about her neighbors who took care of her. They fed her and changed her clothes and stayed with her when she needed company.
>
> We talked for a while and when the time was right, I asked her two questions:
>
> 1. Have you reached the place in your spiritual life that you know for certain that you are going to heaven? She said she did and told me why.
>
> 2. I asked the second question: Suppose you died today and stood before God and He asked you, "Why should I let you into my heaven?" How would you answer that question?
>
> You probably have already guessed her answer to both questions. She loved Jesus and had confessed Him to be her Lord and Savior when she was very young.
>
> We talked a little longer and prayed and as I was leaving, she said the words that I have since carried with me,

everywhere I go: "Now remember, you can always say a good word about Jesus."

You can always say a good word about Jesus. In an elevator, on a plane, in a restaurant, to your children, or spouse— you can always say a good word about Jesus.

That old crippled woman has changed many lives.

"You Can Always Say a Good Word about Jesus"—I love this story. Our words alone can be used to shine for Jesus. In the book of Proverbs there is a verse that talks about how words can be like a honeycomb, sweet to the soul, providing healing to all who hear (Proverbs 16:24). On the other hand, the tongue is like a small flame that has the potential to burn down houses and start forest fires (James 3:5). By being positive, kind, and speaking truth into people's lives, we can have an eternal impact for Jesus.

CREATE OPPORTUNITIES TO SHARE THE GOSPEL!

- Be appreciative to fast-food employees.
- Do not avoid people you know. Simply say hello, and initiate a conversation.
- Help out in the kitchen during the holidays.
- Tithe—you will never ever miss the money you give back to God through the church or world ministries.
- Give your friend a birthday present.
- Buy a souvenir for someone when you visit an interesting place.
- Talk to your hairstylist and the lady who does your nails.
- Be generous to waiters and waitresses.
- Take care of the elderly.

• For me, this one is a challenge: Take out your headphones on the airplane, and strike-up a conversation that may lead to sharing your faith.

Woe to me if I do not preach the gospel.

— 1 Corinthians 9:16

"How much do you have to *hate* somebody to believe everlasting life is possible and not tell them that?" Penn Jillette makes this profound statement on a YouTube video when he experienced receiving a Bible after one of his stand-up comedy acts. The man kindly gave Jillette a copy of the New Testament and spoke kind words. While Jillette's beliefs did not change after this radical encounter, his beliefs on evangelism did. In his YouTube video documentary he compares Christians that do not share the gospel and warn people about hell to allowing a person to commit suicide by jumping off of a bridge.[4] If somebody was unaware they were going to walk off of a cliff then surely you would warn them. As Christians, if we are convicted that Jesus is the only way to get to heaven, we should radically evangelize our faith.

A girl in my Bible study made a comment as to why Christians don't evangelize very often. "Because it makes people uncomfortable," was the girl's statement. I have to ask myself, *Is my momentary comfort more important than somebody else's eternity?* I am selfish in this way, and sometimes choose not to witness to people because I don't want to get the reputation of being *that* person. When I stop and think about it, I realize how silly this is. What better reputation

---

4   https://www.youtube.com/watch?v=6md638smQd8&feature=related.

is there to have than that of sharing God's love and spreading the gospel? Going along with setting our minds on heaven and eternal rewards, I want to store up for myself treasures in heaven. I want to receive the victor's crown in heaven by leading others to Christ here on earth. I want Jesus to say to me someday, "Well done, my good and faithful servant."

Ask yourself these questions and jot down your answers:

1. Who do I know that needs Jesus?

2. What are ways that can I share the good news of Christ's love and reach these people in need?

Don't ever think that God cannot use you. He does not look at what man does; but instead, the Lord looks at the heart (1 Samuel 16:7b). In the same way that the Lord chose David as the anointed one despite his shepherd boy status, the Lord chose you to do great things to further His kingdom. You have the potential to move mountains, make a difference, and even change the world in the name of Jesus. Don't ever rule yourself out of His equation as not good enough, smart enough, or perfect enough. The Lord wants you for His army! He wants to infuse you with the knowledge, wisdom, strength, and perseverance to carry out the purpose He has planned for your life. Even before you were born, the Almighty anointed you, and appointed you as a prophet to the nations (Jeremiah 1:5). Allow the Creator to mold you into His image, and work through your past and present to further His kingdom. Remember, we are equipped for ministry through our experiences. Let God do the steering. By following God's lead, He will reveal His ministry plans for you in His perfect timing. When your goals and God's vision align, He will bless your mission. But when the doors do start opening, don't even pretend like you touched that door handle! Give all of the glory to God. *"But we have this treasure in jars of clay to show that this all-surpassing power is from God and not from us"* (2 Corinthians 4:7).

There is a story in the Bible where Jesus fed five thousand people during one of His sermons. Jesus fed the crowd so that He could continue on with His teachings, and so that they would not have to return home for lunch. With only five loaves of bread and two fish, Jesus was able to feed all of these people. There were even twelve baskets full of leftovers!

> And he directed the people to sit down on the grass. Taking the five loaves and two fish and looking up to heaven, he gave thanks and broke the loaves. Then he gave them to the disciples, and the disciples gave them to the people.
>
> — Matthew 14:19

Before Jesus did any kind of a miracle, he first gave all of the glory to God. By initially thanking His heavenly Father, Jesus acknowledged that the act of the miracle was through God and by His awesome power. In the same way, let us give God the glory first in all that we do.

REDEFINING RELATIONSHIP

Relationship: 1. a connection, association, or involvement. 2. connection between persons by blood or marriage. 3. an emotional or other connection between people (Dictionary.com).

After looking up the definitions of the word relationship, I did not find a strong enough definition to fit the description of my relationship with Jesus Christ, so I made up my own!

> *Relationship (with Jesus)*: 1. The most intimate friendship possible, which is based upon God's infinite love, that needs to be nurtured and valued above all else for the purpose of spiritual growth and discipleship. 2. Being bonded by the blood of Jesus Christ. 3. Unfailing love.

A personal relationship with Christ is like an intentional, nurturing friendship, only much stronger. Jesus will never fail you or abandon you. The Bible calls us to trust in this promise and be strong and brave because of it. "Be strong and courageous. Do not be afraid or terrified because of them, for the Lord your God goes with you; he will never leave you nor forsake you" (Deuteronomy 31:6). I find so much reassurance, comfort, and love in this verse. Unlike people in this world, a relationship with Christ will never disappoint us. If you have already accepted Jesus into your heart as your personal Lord and Savior, make Him a priority in your life. Go to Him in prayer and trust in His promises. Give your anxieties and worldly troubles to the Lord through prayer and petition. Share your heart with Jesus.

When I was a little girl, four years old, my older brothers, Tate and Austin, and their friends, dug a hole in the backyard with shovels. This was when my family lived in Midland, Texas. Obviously, there wasn't much to do in this small city of West Texas, so my brothers found entertainment in digging a large hole in the ground. Over time, the hole in the backyard kept getting wider and deeper to the point that I was afraid of falling in because I knew I wouldn't be able to get out on my own. One day, I became a little too adventurous and thought that the pit would be a fun play place. It was a trap. After climbing down, I realized I couldn't get back up, and I began screaming and crying for help. To this day, I still remember panicking in that pit. Eventually, my dad heard my cries, reached into the dark place where I was stuck, and pulled me to the earth's surface. Despite my parent's warnings and advice to stay out of the hole, I had to learn through personal experience. Isn't it funny how this precedent holds true for many life scenarios. People may give us excellent advice, but sometimes we have to experience the pitfall ourselves to truly learn and grow. But the good news is that our heavenly Father can always pull us back up.

Falling into a pit can be a scary deal. As humans and followers of Christ, we are not always sure what the Lord is up to in our lives. When we fall into a spiritual, financial, or relational pit, our situation can seem despondent. After I broke up with my boyfriend of three years, I felt stuck in an impossibly deep pit. Like my four-year-old self, I was lost and needed help getting out. There were many tears during this time of sadness, but I eventually reached for God's hand, which was there all along, and He pulled me back up.

There is an old fable about a donkey and a farmer, which demonstrates the concept of a pitfall in a relatable way. Being stuck in a pit can cause panic, confusion, and loss of hope. "Shake It Off and Take a Step Up" is a message of hope that looks at falling into a pit through a different lens.

"SHAKE IT OFF AND TAKE A STEP UP"
(AUTHOR UNKNOWN)

One day a farmer's donkey fell into an abandoned well. The animal cried piteously for hours as the farmer tried to figure out what to do. Finally, he decided the animal was old and the well needed to be covered up anyway; so it just wasn't worth it to him to try to retrieve the donkey.

He invited all his neighbors to come over and help him. They each grabbed a shovel and began to shovel dirt into the well. Realizing what was happening, the donkey at first cried and wailed horribly. Then, a few shovelfuls later, he quieted down completely.

The farmer peered down into the well, and was astounded by what he saw. With every shovelful of dirt that hit his back, the donkey was doing something amazing. He would shake it off and take a step up on the new layer of dirt. As the farmer's neighbors continued to shovel dirt on top of the animal, he would shake it off and take a step up.

Pretty soon, the donkey stepped up over the edge of the well and trotted off, to the shock and astonishment of all the neighbors. Life is going to shovel dirt on you, all kinds of dirt. The trick to getting out of the well is to not let it bury you, but to shake it off and take a step up. Each of our troubles is a stepping-stone.

When I am going through a tough situation, I pray that God would either a) change my circumstances, or b) change my perspective. Although my breakup was a heart-wrenching period in my life, I never will regret my pitfall because of all of the valuable lessons l learned throughout my getting unstuck. We all stumble. We all fall short of the glory of God. I am not perfect, and will never be. I have messed up and will continue to mess up so many more times in my life. I stumble in and out of sin, but through it all I have learned the secret of how to get back up, and press on towards the prize. "Each of our troubles is a stepping-stone." Once we discover that one act of disobedience has the ability to be turned into a step up rather than a shovel of dirt, only then can we become living testimonies to others in Jesus' name. Even when we are puzzled about how God is working in our lives, God will never leave us. All the while it feels as if dirt is being thrown upon our backs, God will never forsake us. He will always provide a way out, and teach us ways to shake it off and take a step up.

Jesus Christ paid the price. When we do fall into a pit, and our situation seems that of a spiritual death, the Lord is a loving farmer who wants to save us from the pitfall of our sins through Jesus' ultimate sacrifice. He died a horrible death on a cross, so that we might be saved by grace. Next time you have fallen and the getting up seems impossible, don't you dare give up because Jesus' love is relentless. Our heavenly Father's hand will always be outstretched to pull you out of the pit. Simply take hold of His hand, and accept the free gift of a personal relationship with Jesus Christ.

My favorite song is "Beautiful Things," by Gungor. This song speaks biblical truth and sheds light on the nature of our Creator's abounding mercy and grace. The Lord God wants to use you to spread His word. Rise up and shine God's love.

BEAUTIFUL THINGS (GUNGOR)

All this pain
I wonder if I'll ever find my way
I wonder if my life could really change at all
All this earth
Could all that is lost ever be found
Could a garden come up from this ground at all

You make beautiful things
You make beautiful things out of the dust
You make beautiful things
You make beautiful things out of us

All around
Hope is springing up from this old ground
Out of chaos life is being found in You

You make beautiful things
You make beautiful things out of the dust
You make beautiful things
You make beautiful things out of us.[5]

The Lord does make beautiful things out of us! By allowing God to take over our hearts and souls with His all-consuming love, something that was once broken can be made new. By the power of His divine touch in our lives, God can make us new creations.

PRAYER:

Lord God, You make beautiful things. Mold me into something beautiful. Make me new. I pray that my actions and desires would please You. I pray that I would flee from all sinful desires of this world. I want to honor You in word

---

5   Lisa Gungor, Michael Gungor, *Beautiful Things*. worshiptogether.com, 2009.

and deed. Help me to become more bold in my faith, and spread Your love to others by not only living as a Christian example, but also by being intentional and speaking Your truth. Show me ways that I can live for You, and share my faith each day, Jesus. It's in Your holy name I pray. Amen.

CHAPTER SIX

BUILD A BOAT

Above all else, guard your heart for it is the wellspring of life.
— Proverbs 4:23

MUSIC, TV SHOWS, BOOKS, MAGAZINES, chick flicks, Pinterest wedding pages, relationship statuses on Facebook . . . romance is in the air. Romance is virtually everywhere! In a relationship-flooded society, we must learn how to guard our hearts and guide our minds through the eye of the storm to keep from being consumed with this "significant other" mentality.

Learning how to decipher between living *in* the world versus living *of* the world is a spiritual skill. What is my soul consuming is the first question we must ask ourselves. Are we constantly feeding it junk food in the form of gossip magazines, steamy romance novels, relationship-focused music, and TV shows that involve impure relationships? Or are we guarding our hearts and our minds in Christ Jesus? Learning to watch and monitor everything our eyes and ears consume is crucial to our spiritual wellbeing.

I happen to love music. I really enjoy listening to good music, even secular music. I am a fan of artists and groups such as Carrie Underwood, Taylor Swift, Gavin DeGraw, Jack Johnson, Train, Rascal Flatts, and many others. Nothing's wrong with secular music. God created music for our enjoyment and entertainment; but more importantly, He created it as a form of worship, to bring glory to His name.

While I like secular music and listen to it often, I try to keep it clean and mix it up with Christian jams as well. By listening to messages that speak truth, a sense of hope overflows into our life situations. Truth means that the messages align with the Bible, God's word. Avoiding songs that send messages that are unhealthy to our emotional wellbeing, and feed us lies, can protect our spiritual wellbeing, which is our relationship with Christ. By listening to songs that are positive and uplifting, our emotional wellbeing, which is our state of joy and peace, can also be protected.

A question that I like to ask myself when I'm listening to music in the car is, *"Would I be playing this song if Jesus were in the passenger's seat?"* Similar questions can be asked for other forms of eye/ear consumption. These questions relate to daily living in the form of watching movies, reading magazines, and participating in social media.

Movies: *Would Jesus agree to go see this movie with me?*

Magazines: *Am I relying more on this magazine or God's Word for advice?*

Social Media: *Should I spend an extra fifteen minutes on Facebook or Instagram, or should I use this spare time to get into God's Word?*

When I was a little girl, about ten years old, I remember taking my little Bichon Frisé puppy named Sophie for a walk in the neighborhood. I had her on a leash, but my ten-year-old little mind wondered if Sophie would obediently stay by my side if I took off the leash. It seemed like a good idea at the time, so I set her free! After a matter of seconds, Sophie was darting down the middle of the street into oncoming traffic. It was a tight race between my ten-year-old self and the six-month-old puppy, but eventually I did catch Sophie.

Using this story in comparison to my emotions, I know that they have to be kept on a leash too. We can't let our emotions run wild and free because it is dangerous. It is perilous to our mental and spiritual health. Sometimes our thoughts can seem harmless and innocent, but without keeping them under restraint, our emotions have the ability to run wild. In the same way we want to protect our puppy, we are called to guard our hearts above all else. This starts with protecting our minds by keeping our emotions in check. As women, we are emotional creatures. It is easy to become captivated with the idea of being in a relationship or having a boyfriend. (I am guilty.) Our greatest resistant for guarding our hearts in the society we live in is learning how to control our emotions through Christ Jesus. In doing this, there are so many roadblocks that we have to watch for and avoid along the way.

We live in a romance-crazed society that constantly idolizes the idea of being in a relationship. Not only is the idea of a relationship stressed, but also it is stressed in a present-tense sort of way. If you are not in a relationship *now* then you are worthless. These are the lies Satan feeds us. When we take a look at the Bible and see what

God's Word has to offer, the story of Noah demonstrates the wisdom of a man who breaks societal norms in order to protect himself and his family from destruction.

Noah was a man after God's own heart. In a society that was flooded in sin, Noah found favor in the eyes of the Lord. The Earth was so corrupt at the time that God decided He would destroy it completely. Among the people of the world, Noah was the only righteous man, and for this reason alone, the Lord spared Noah and his family. Our God is just. There is a repetitive pattern in the Bible where Noah was obedient to the Lord. Long before a single drop of rain fell from the sky, God gave Noah specific instructions to build an ark. He gave Noah the dimensions for the ark, the list of food and supplies needed, and the directions for which animals would live on the boat during the upcoming flood. "Noah did everything just as God commanded him" (Genesis 6:22). Three times, this verse exists throughout the story in Genesis of Noah and the flood, which destroyed life on Earth. *Noah did everything just as God commanded him.* The story of Noah serves as a prime example of how God's mercy rains down on the obedient.

God saved Noah and his entire family. Why? He was obedient to God. Noah was a spiritual leader. He led by example of walking faithfully with the Lord. Naturally, when we are passionate about something, we talk about it! I'm sure Noah had intentional conversations with his family about God and spoke of Him often.

Noah saved his entire family from the flood. When we apply Noah's precedent to our own lives, we have to not only think about saving ourselves from the flood but also, we must consider those around us. Who can I save from the flood? Are my actions leading someone to Christ and away from the "boyfriend mentality," or are my actions detrimental to a non-Christian looking for a safe haven? By staying afloat in a relationship-flooded society, we have the potential to help save our family and friends.

To be perfectly honest, there have been times in my life where I have fallen short in this area and have let my life become swamped with an unhealthy relationship orientation. I look back and think about others I drug down to the marshes with me. This being said, I know that there have been moments in my life and opportunities where I have succeeded in an evangelical way by being like Noah, a spiritual leader. Our words and actions influence others way more than we think. They have the potential to either drown us, and everyone we know, or to lead people to the ark of deliverance, Jesus Christ!

The beginning of my breakup experience, I was in an emotionally vulnerable state, and suspect you might be too. By becoming aware of our thoughts, we have the ability to capture our weak, vulnerable, wrongly focused emotions and surrender our every thought over to God, who has the ability to redirect and fortify them as lovely, pure, and pleasing in His sight (Philippians 4:8). Memorizing Scripture has really helped me to learn how to forfeit my boyfriend-indulgent desires over to the Lord. Prayer and listening to music that does not feed these desires is salient for me to fight the urge to feel sorry for myself in my loneliness. While it's okay to be lonely, it's not okay to mope and be so inwardly focused that our own ministry is crippled. We were set on this earth for a purpose. One of the best ways to stay afloat in this relationship-flooded society is to focus on the needs of others more than the needs of ourselves.

Jesus will deliver us from the storm. He asks only that we remain faithful, and let God do the rest. This standard of faithfulness covers a broad spectrum. It entails the conditions of our hearts; our intentions, our words, and actions that influence others; investing time in other peoples' lives; being well-attuned, good listeners that offer sound advice when necessary; serving people in everyday life; and mentoring younger girls.

The conditions of our hearts can be made pure by aligning our actions with what we learn from the Bible, from sermons, and through prayer. Intentions are a heart's reflection. When our intentions are evil (not of the Lord), we need to surrender our selfish ambitions over to God and pray for Him to reset our mentality. This is a continuous act of prayer. In order to keep my heart and actions aligned with the Lord's vision, I constantly must keep praying to become a woman after God's own heart. This entails sharing with God my struggles, desires, fears, hopes, and dreams. I listen to God's response through the Bible, the echo of the Spirit, and wise counsel—pastors, mentors, my family, and Christian friends.

Our actions reflect our intentions and our intentions reflect our innermost desires. When our most important and urgent desire is to please the Lord, everything else in our life falls into its rightful place, priorities are aligned, and the conditions of our hearts are purified and made holy by His grace.

SIGNIFICANCE, MATERIAL POSSESSIONS, AFFIRMATION

These are three big things that we as women struggle with. Take Eve in the garden of Eden for example. Eve wanted to become like God (significance), the fruit looked pleasing to her eye (material possessions), and the serpent told her she should eat it (affirmation). The serpent knew just where to strike. Because of not being able to withstand these alluring temptations, Eve sinned against God and ate the Fruit of the Knowledge of Good and Evil. She even took the affirmation a step further and gave Adam some of it. Any one or combination of these three idols can separate us from having the most intimate relationship possible with God.

1. Significance: Would you rather invest in an old jalopy of a car, or a brand-new vehicle that provides perfect directions and is equipped with an eternal warranty? Well, duh—the new car! Finding your significance in Christ is like the new car. It is everlasting, never gets old, and is equipped with directions in the form of the Bible. The story from the Bible about the wise man who built his house upon the rock represents a man who found his significance in God, and lived his life with eternity in mind. The storms came, the rain poured, and the waves crashed, but his house stood firm upon the Rock (Matthew 7:24-27).

2. Material Possessions: Time and money are two big factors that indicate one's life priorities. In this way consider some of the things you value most in your life. Clothes, shoes, cool cars, house, laptop, cell phone, Facebook—I know that I am guilty! Let us rethink how we spend our time and money, because if all of these things are all based on material things then we are wasting our time chasing after the world rather than storing up for ourselves treasures in heaven. Write below where most of your time and money is spent.

_____

_____

3. Affirmation: WWJT! Remember those cool WWJD bracelets you used to wear growing up? Change the letter D to a T and you get the word "think." Acknowledge the question, "What Would Jesus Think?" when considering whose opinion really matters. In an image-focused society, it is hard to not care about what others think. But as Christians, we are called to a higher standard. Relying solely on God's opinion takes practice through mental and intentional acts of discipline; but by refocusing our eyes on heavenly matters, it is easier to consider God's opinion over peoples' without hesitation. We are not citizens on earth, but rather our citizenship is in heaven (Philippians 3:20).

As Christ followers we will face persecution. This means not everyone that you encounter is going to like you, or give you the stamp of approval, but that is okay! Our self-worth comes from the one whose opinion trumps all else, the ace of spades, the Lord Jesus Christ.

Which area do you see yourself struggling most with? Write down which one applies to you most, and briefly explain ways you see yourself striving in this particular way. Jot down why you think you are having a difficult time with this area of your life.

_____

_____

PRAYER:

God, I am struggling with significance [my example]. I need You to help me realize that my identity is found in You, and You alone. Lord, I surrender this need of feeling significant to You. Show me ways to do this, God. I want to feel fully secure and confident in knowing I have You in my life as my number one priority. You are my rock God. I love You and need You, Lord. Help me in this area of my life. It's in Jesus' mighty name I pray. Amen.

We've got to build a boat! Saying no to slippery sin is so much easier said than done. By being proactive and recognizing where these traps can occur, where these sins stem from, and why, we can build a boat and protect ourselves from the storm of Satan's lies. Like Noah, if we are able to listen to God and do what He says, we are assured safety. "The Lord is a refuge for the oppressed, a stronghold in times of trouble" (Psalm 9:9).

Sink or swim. In order to be Jesus' hands and feet, we've got to dive into society and be a part of people's lives. At the same time, we are called to a higher standard of living and must learn how to swim. What separates Christians and non-Christians? Hopefully, our daily lives—our compassionate hearts, joyful spirits, and habits of forgiveness—draw a fine line. But let's make it evident to all who we stand for starting with the little things. By changing our intake, our output becomes that much clearer.

We have the ability to teach others how to swim with us. Living radical lives for Christ and being bold in our faith can really affect the way people view Christianity. By becoming passionate Christ followers, others might want to know what we are doing and why. Actions speak louder than words. The way we live our lives for Christ can have an eternal impact in the lives of others. It may even cause the people around us to want to seek the Ark of Refuge, our Savior, Jesus Christ.

Building an ark takes years and years. This is why it is so important that we have strong Christian friends in our lives. With the help of other Christ followers encouraging us in our faith, holding us accountable, and pushing us to live life with higher standards, building a boat becomes a much easier thing to do.

CHAPTER SEVEN

TRAINING YOUR EAR

I HAVE BROWN SUGAR, FLOUR, baking soda, chocolate chips, food coloring, sprinkles, cookie cutters, and cupcake sleeves all in my pantry. I have muffin pans, cake holders, and cookie sheets all in my kitchen drawers. I have all of the right supplies, yet I don't bake often. If you take a close look at all of my ingredients, you may find that they are expired, and my pans are shiny like new. I choose to go to the grocery store and simply pick up a vegetable tray or an already-made box of cookies for parties and other social events. Sometimes I will even go the extra mile, take the cookies out of their plastic tin, and put them on a decorative plate, or in a festive plastic bucket. While I am in no way condemning those fellow nonbakers out there who are like me, I am simply using an analogy.

I know exactly how to make things appear like I have everything in my life all together. Sometimes I even feel this way about my relationship with Christ. All of the essential ingredients to make something delicious are stored in my pantry, but I refuse to apply them towards a homemade recipe. It takes time, and dedication, to make a homemade dessert. In this same way, applying biblical principles to my life is a discipline. I could stand up on a podium all day, and give you the exact recipe to be a "perfect" Christian. But the reality is that all Christians fall short of the glory of God. No matter how hard we try, we will continue to sin even after we are saved, so there really is no "perfect" Christian recipe except Christ Himself! At the same time, we are called to strive daily towards becoming more like Christ, and our recipe is the Bible. In relation to this, being a Christian is like NIKE: Just Do It—live for Him.

Applying biblical principles to my life is so much easier said than done. Sometimes I would much rather cheat and simply make my life look legitimate externally, but the Lord does not look at things man does; the Lord looks at the heart (1 Samuel 16:7). This being said, God wants our hearts to be sold out for Jesus. It does not please Him when we sin, but His blood covers the multitude of our sins. By His grace we are saved (Ephesians 2:8). God is a loving Father who is more concerned that our souls are in full submission to Him, than with our sins. This is because He wants our hearts. The Lord wants the conditions of our hearts to be so in love with Jesus that we want to follow His commands. We want to go to church and learn more about our King. We want to read His word and worship Him. God can easily determine the homemade baked goods versus the store-bought goods. But, being a homemade cookie is more than appearing righteous externally. The Pharisees made it their goal to appear flawless in the public's eye. Because of their selfish ambitions, Jesus condemned them. The Lord wants our hearts and souls to be mindfully His. God wants the wellsprings of my life to overflow with love, praise, and thanksgiving for Jesus Christ, my saving grace, my personal Lord and Savior. Only then can my life be a true reflection of Christ's love.

Recently, I read Lysa Terkeurst's book, *The Best Yes*. This book helped me look at everyday life through a whole new lens, and changed my attitude to that of "Bring it on!" God sometimes challenges us with things in life that may seem like intimidating tasks, or things we simply don't want to do. In fact, these might even be things we don't want to *stop* doing, or let go of. The power of a kind no is also a "Best Yes." Yes or no, it's about learning to listen to the Holy Spirit inside of us, in order to make God-fearing decisions. As one wise woman explained to me, the term "God-fearing" simply means to hold the opinion of the Lord God in the highest of regards. By continuously seeking an awareness and knowledge of our Father's thoughts on our actions, we have the ability to make right decisions. This is the heart behind *The Best Yes*.

In my women's Bible study, one girl made a comment that struck a funny chord within me and inspired me to protest. The girl's comment was in regards to helping the homeless. She admitted that sometimes she is hesitant about helping homeless people or those in need, because they are not always being truthful about their situation. "You just hear of those stories where the homeless person drives away in a fancy car." This has been true in some rare cases, and it reminds me of the Sherlock Holmes book *The Man With the Twisted Lip*. This book is about a homeless person who is an imposter and is actually well off. He receives a decent income and is able to make a living and support his family by street begging, but at the same time, he lives under the burden of being a fake and even hiding this secret from his wife and family. In the end, the police catch him, and his true identity is revealed. It is a heartbreaking scene in the book when his wife discovers the truth. She is virtually crushed.

In regards to the girl's statement about not always being willing to help the homeless because of their need for help being potentially fake, I responded: "Sometimes the Holy Spirit calls us to do something, and moves in our hearts and souls in such a way that we know that we are supposed to do something as an act to further the kingdom." The Lord's tugging on our hearts can be felt, and the more we learn to respond to that pull, saying yes, the easier it is to know when the Lord is specifically calling us to complete a task. We can become stronger witnesses of Christ to others if we learn to listen for His voice. His voice is an echo in your soul, the calling to live above worldly standards. It is a God-placed, urgent desire to go against our sinful human nature in a particular way, at a specific point in time. We have all felt this tugging on our hearts. Christ commands us to listen, and surrender to His pull, forfeiting our selfish ways of living in order to carry out the will of God.

While I want to condemn those homeless impostors and have a self-righteous attitude, I have to stop and think about my flaws, because when I really think about it, I am an imposter too. Many times I have a said one thing about my faith, but done the opposite. I fall short of the glory of God time after time again, so who am I to judge another's sins? No, I must first remove the plank out of my own eye (Matthew 7:5).

The process of "training your ear" is a musical term that refers to the ability to hear music and in turn be able to play simply by listening. Being able to listen to a song and know the exact pitch of each separate note takes practice. Talented musicians are able to create beautiful masterpieces by culminating various rhythms, patterns, and chords just after hearing a simple melody.

As Christ followers, we are called to train our hearts. When we hear the calling of the Spirit, asking us gently to help someone or become more like Jesus in some specific way, we have two options: to listen and obey, or to ignore the echo of the Spirit inside of us. When we choose to listen and obey, our ears become more open and available to what Christ has to say. We are better able to hear what He is speaking into our lives. When we choose to ignore the voice of the Spirit, His echo inside of us grows fainter and becomes more distant.

I saw an angel inside of the grocery store once. Milk, bread, cottage cheese, cookie dough, juice, cheese, and apples were all that was on my list; and I was trying to stay within a strict budget. As I approached the checkout station, I rolled my cart into the closest line. When I glanced over at checkout station number three, I noticed a little old lady in tattered clothing who had only a few items in her basket and was proceeding to the checkout. After my quick observation, I switched over into the shorter line. The little old lady in front of me reminded me of my sweet great-grandmother, Joannie, who is ninety-four years old. She most certainly had some years under her belt, and I couldn't help but think to myself, *This poor lady should not still have to do her own grocery shopping.* She was staring at the register screen intently when her last item, grapes, rang up.

"Your total is twenty-four dollars and fifty-seven cents," the cashier announced.

"I thought these grapes were two ninety-nine," said the old lady, despondently.

"Per pound," insisted the cashier.

Reluctantly, the little old woman replied, "Okay, I can't get them then. This is all I have." She pulled out several wadded dollar bills.

This episode in front of me absolutely broke my heart. At that moment, I heard a small voice inside of my soul that was telling me that I could do something about the situation. I tried to ignore it at first because I was on a budget. *Surely this woman's grapes will put me over,* I said to myself. *After all, it's not my responsibility* (one of Satan's lies). When the nudging inside of me became stronger, I began to actually consider the Holy Spirit's proposition. Then I began to wonder, *What if this woman is really an angel in disguise?* I doubted this notion. *But I don't want to embarrass her and she is about to walk off anyway.* I had a quick decision to make. Would I choose to be complacent, or go out on a limb?

"Ma'am, I want to buy those lady's grapes for her," I told the cashier.

That choice later became one of the best decisions of my entire week! As the cashier handed the little old lady her grapes and told her that someone had purchased them for her, I saw her face brilliantly light up with joy and thanksgiving. I still to this day think that little old lady with tattered clothing, and short, curly salt-and-pepper hair might have been an angel.

When we choose to bless others, God blesses us. The three dollars I spent on those grapes that day helped someone in need, and demonstrated God's love. I have never missed that money, and know I never will. Being stingy in life with one's time, money, kind words, love, or attention is useless, but being a cheerful giver is absolutely priceless.

Each of you should give what you have decided in your heart to give, not reluctantly or under compulsion, for God loves a cheerful giver.

— 2 Corinthians 9:7

I learned something else that day too: Had I not done anything to help the little old lady, the world would have kept revolving around the sun and spinning on its axis, yes; but out of my complacency, a wrong decision would have been made. Had I heard the Holy Spirit inside of me, and then decided to not listen and obey, that would have been in fact my decision. I think that in some instances it is better to have a hands-off approach, but when it comes to helping others in need that does not hold true. Although I have missed chances and opportunities to obey the Holy Spirit's cries to help others, I have learned that missing those special opportunities leaves you feeling empty inside, with a sense of purposelessness. I have to remind myself time and time again, complacency is a decision. When we know and can recognize the Holy Spirit's echo inside of us asking us to rise up and demonstrate who and what we stand for, more than likely it is because it is a window of opportunity to love and to be Jesus to others.

Make a list of all the ways you feel the Holy Spirit tugging at your heart.

Here's my list:

WAYS I FEEL THE HOLY SPIRIT TUGGING AT MY HEART

- Go on a mission trip to Africa this Christmas.
- Volunteer in the community.
- Give God all the glory in writing this book.
- Become a teacher when I graduate.
- Stop striving and start thriving in Him!.

CHAPTER EIGHT

FROG

I get knocked down
But I get up again
You're never gonna keep me down[6]

IF YOU'VE EVER LISTENED TO the song "Tubthumping" by Chumbawamba, then you understand the enthusiasm of the challenge to get back up again in whatever life circumstance. This song is widely used as a pump-up song for athletes, and was featured in the Nintendo *FIFA: Road to World Cup 1998* video game. During my childhood, my older brother Austin owned this game, so naturally the theme song has been drilled into my brain. I used to dance and jump around to this song in between the soccer video games while my brother selected his team, players, and opponent. Austin also would listen to "Tubthumping" before his own Southlake Carroll High School soccer games. While this song has the ability to get athletes excited and ready to play, the Bible also can have this ability in a different sense. God's Word is an enabler for Christians to live life to the fullest. I experience a spiritual high after I spend quality time

---

6   Chumbawamba, *Tubthumping*. EMI Group Limited/Universal Records, 1997.

with the Lord. This spiritual high rejuvenates me throughout the day and reminds me of why I am here on this earth. God has given me a purpose. Although I do not know His exact plans for my life, I do know that in all of my endeavors, I am supposed to be a vessel for Jesus Christ by demonstrating His love and bringing glory to God. Even when I do fall down, and mess up, it is important that I get back up again, and never let Satan keep me down.

Looking at the life of Moses, it is evident that he was a vessel for God. Here's the story of Moses in a nutshell:.

During the time of Pharaoh's decree to kill all Hebrew baby boys, Moses was placed in a basket as an infant and carried across the Nile River where the queen of Egypt found and raised him. Moses grew up as a prince of Egypt, not knowing he was actually grafted into the royal family. When Moses discovered the truth about his roots, it was hard for him to watch his people suffer as slaves under the wrath of Pharaoh. Eventually, Moses ran away to the desert where he found a clan of God-fearing people. These people accepted him into their community and Moses ended up marrying one of the leader's daughters. Moses' first encounter with God was through a burning bush. This is when the Lord first revealed Himself, spoke to Moses, and commanded him to return to Egypt to free the Israelites, God's chosen people. Although Moses was fearful, he returned to Egypt where he commanded Pharaoh to let his people go. Belligerent, Pharaoh refused to free the Israelites from captivity. In turn, the Lord inflicted a series of plagues upon Egypt. It was not until God took away the firstborn of every Egyptian household that Pharaoh realized the finality of the situation: God would have His way. Again, Moses commanded

Pharaoh to let his people go. After much reluctance, Pharaoh finally agreed, and Moses began to boldly lead the Israelites away from Egypt. They traveled as far as the Red Sea before Pharaoh changed his mind and sent an army after the Israelites. God in turn parted the Red Sea, and Moses led his people across. As the Egyptians tried to cross the parted sea in pursuit of their former slaves, God released His grip on the waters and the waves came tumbling down, consuming the Egyptian army. Israel was free. Moses held tight to God's promise, and because of his faithfulness, God gave Moses authority and leadership over the Israelites. God gave Moses the Ten Commandments to give to Israel, and even led God's people up until the threshold of the Promised Land. The Lord was able to use Moses as a vessel because he lived his life as a FROG: Fully Relying On God.

In my daily walk with Christ, the phrase Fully Rely On God (FROG) has helped me to remember to depend on God in whatever challenge I am facing. During my second and last year of graduate school at the University of Tulsa, I found myself at a crossroads. For six years of my life, I had been training to become an educator. My undergraduate degree is in Elementary Education, and I was about to complete my Master's degree in Math and Science Education. Despite all of my training, I was not sure if I wanted to become a teacher. Teachers are typically overworked, underpaid, not appreciated, and always running on empty. This was my perspective at least. When I took the time to pray about the direction of my life and asked God to reveal His plans for my life, God humbled me in regards to my attitude about becoming a teacher. I began to look at all of the positive aspects of becoming a teacher: summers off, shorter work days, serving as a role model and impacting kids' lives, affecting young students' futures. There's even a cherry on top of the sundae! I can write and work on my books during my summers off. God gave me a resounding peace about His will for me to teach. In regards to becoming a teacher, I am choosing to FROG and trust in the Lord, knowing that He has a divine plan.

God wants us to be FROGs. Just like Moses, God wants to use us for His plans and purposes. As Christians, we have been grafted into the family of God (Colossians 2:11). We are daughters of the Lord Most High. Of all of the leadership positions and things that I have been entrusted with, this is my greatest honor and privilege of them all. When I consider some of the worldly privileges in my life, I can more tangibly relate to what some the expectations are of the greatest privilege—being a daughter of Christ.

I was a graduate teaching assistant at the University of Tulsa for a year and a half. This has been one of my most esteemed honors. Each day of work, I would wear business casual clothing, and would show up on time. I always made an attempt to help the professors to the best of my ability in whatever ways possible. What are some of the greatest honors or privileges in your life? What are some of the mandates and requirements that come along with this privilege?

Let's think of this esteemed honor as an analogy in comparison to being a woman of God. You might be wondering, *What are some of my expectations as a Christian? What am I supposed to wear? How am I supposed to act? Who am I supposed to help? How am I supposed to think?* All of these are great questions that are answered throughout the Bible.

Modest is hottest! As women of God, we are supposed to look the part. By this I mean that we are supposed to dress appropriately and not wear skimpy outfits, but also we are supposed to take pride in our appearance. Taking care of our bodies and being faithful in regards to exercise and what we eat are imperative to reflecting Christ's image. The Creator of the universe fearfully and wonderfully made us in His image (Psalm 139:14). Let's take pride in that!

We are called to love God and love people. Jesus Himself said that the first and greatest commandment is to love God with everything in us, and the second is to love our neighbor as ourselves (Matthew 22:36-39).

There is a motto that I learned growing up that was drilled into my brain during the nine summers I attended Kanakuk Camps: "I am third." This phrase stands for putting God first, others second, and myself third. While this standard is easier said than done, this is how we are to live as Christ followers.

Finally, brothers and sisters, whatever is true, whatever is noble, whatever is right, whatever is pure, whatever is lovely, whatever is admirable—if anything is excellent or praiseworthy—think about such things.
— Philippians 4:8

Living the "I am third" lifestyle begins with our mentality. Our actions reflect the conditions our hearts. By thinking pure thoughts and considering God-honoring ways, our intentions and motivations will begin to reflect the will of God. The "I am third" lifestyle does not come naturally because we are sinful beings, but as Christians we are called to a greater caliber of love and sacrifice, to that of Jesus Christ. The Bible has the ability to transform and to renew our minds. Only by resetting our focus on Christ can we avoid the pitfall of being conformed to the patterns of this world (Romans 12:2).

DEFYING GRAVITY

Growing up I did gymnastics, and starting in middle school, I began my cheerleading career. I cheered on a competitive squad during seventh and eighth grade. Our team name was the Crusaders, and we went by the motto, "Crusaders for Christ." Our coach was a police officer who had cheered in college. Mike was a godly man who led by example and was always dedicated to improving our squad. Because of having a wonderful coach, I was a good cheerleader. My toe touches were high, my voice was loud, I was always smiling, and I had beautiful backhand springs. My junior year of high school, I tried out for the varsity cheerleading squad. During the tryout, I ended up not doing quite as well as I had hoped, but I was one of two girls trying out who could actually tumble, so I still had hope. As we were handed a letter of either acceptance or rejection onto the squad, butterflies were fluttering everywhere in my body. I ran out to my car and ripped open the letter. It said something short and sweet, along the lines of, *Thank you for trying out for the varsity cheerleading squad. We're sorry to say that you did not make it, but please try out again next year.* I couldn't believe it, and I didn't understand. I was devastated.

Although I was a really good cheerleader, a bad tryout had ruined my chances. I ran cross-country for the school that year instead, but kept doing competitive cheerleading outside of school. Private practice after private practice, I worked so hard to earn my standing back tuck, and get the rest of my skills up to par. The next year, I tried out for the varsity cheerleading squad again. With a standing back tuck under my belt, and my other skills perfected, I made it!

The next year I decided to attend the University of Tulsa for college. I tried out to be a college cheerleader for TU and made the squad. Remembering my experience of failure in high school, tears of joy streamed down my face when I saw my tryout number posted to the door on the list of the new squad members.

Trust in the Lord with all your heart and lean not on your own understanding; in all your ways acknowledge him, and he will make your paths straight.
— Proverbs 3:5-6

God taught me many hard lessons throughout my cheerleading career. I would not have become a college cheerleader had I not experienced the failure of not making the squad my junior year of high school. Had I not been faced with adversity, I would not have put in the hard work and effort it required for me to be the very best cheerleader I could be. Little did I know that during the time of cheer tryouts my junior year, God had bigger plans for me that went even beyond high school cheer. The most powerful life lesson I learned throughout the ups and downs of cheerleading was to trust in the Lord no matter what. He was, and is always up to something that may be out of sight, and sometimes beyond our ability to understand at the time, but His purposes are so much greater than the temporary hurts and struggles we've all experienced.

God is like the force of gravity. We cannot beat the most powerful force in the universe! By defying gravity, we are really only prolonging the inevitable. In the same way, God's will for my life prevails and His purposes remain, despite any opposition. When I really think about it, gravity works in my favor, and I would never want it to fail me anyways. Gravity keeps the universe in order. It makes human life possible. In the same way, God wants only good things for our lives.

> *And we know that in all things God works for the good of those*
> *who love him, who have been called according to his purpose.*
> — Romans 8:28

God reveals His awesome power through His divine plan for my life. His plans always end up playing out exactly the way He intended. When I choose to FROG, God allows wonderful things to happen to me—things beyond my horizons of understanding, things that I could never have even imagined possible.

There's a saying at my church that goes like this:

Pastor: *"God is good . . ."*

Church body: *"All the time!"*

Pastor: *"And all the time . . ."*

Church body: *"God is good!"*

I love reciting these words at the end of a service. These words empower me to live my life in full surrender to the Lord. As I leave church, these words encourage me in my faith, and give me boldness and strength to follow Christ wholeheartedly and to be Jesus' hands and feet to a hurting world in need of His love and mercy.

PRAYER:

Lord, help me to fully rely on You in all things. Show me ways to reach other people for You. Give me confidence that I would never shy away from being proud of my identity found in You. Like mirrors reflect the sun, let me exude Your brilliant light. Show me how to feed Your sheep Jesus. It's in Your precious and holy name I pray. Amen.

CHAPTER NINE

PRAYER WARRIORS

"IF OUR GOD IS FOR us, then who could ever stop us? And if our God is with us, then what could stand against?" The words to the song "Our God" echoed in the room as I prayed[7]. I cried out to God that He would guide my new life, and guide my new relationship with Daniel. I was struggling with overcoming the past, the shame and guilt from my old life. There was a new man in my life that was becoming a good friend and slowly winning my heart. Daniel loved Jesus with all of his heart, and our season of being friends who simply played tennis together was slowly changing. God was working in our relationship and doing good things. Yet, I still felt so defeated.

I struggled. I struggled with starting over. Mentally, there was a subconscious notion telling me that I would never find love again. I told myself that things would never amount to my previous relationship. I pushed Daniel away. I prolonged our friendship and when we did begin to date, I freaked out and ended things almost immediately. Throughout this emotional roller coaster, I did not seek God in prayer. I did not ask God about His plans or His intentions for my life in the

---

7   Chris Tomlin, *Our God*. Sixsteprecords, 2010.

area of a romantic relationship, and a potential future spouse. Instead, I relied on my emotions. God soon reminded me of Jeremiah 17:9: "The heart is deceitful above all things and beyond cure. Who can understand it?"

After disappearing from Daniel's life and ignoring him for a few weeks, I felt a tugging at my heart to call him and talk about some things. This verse weighed heavy on my heart, and there was a conviction in my mind that Daniel had all of the qualities I was looking for in a future spouse. He was a Christian leader, trustworthy, chivalrous, not easily angered, intellectual, hardworking, and he deeply cared about me. On top of all of that, I knew that he would be a wonderful dad to his kids someday. When I pulled up my "Husband List" on my iPhone notes app, I was shocked to find that Daniel met and exceeded all of the criteria listed. This list was recorded long before Daniel stepped into my life.

HUSBAND LIST

- Christian
- Trust
- Spiritual Leader
- Gentleman
- Good Dad Someday
- Not Easily Angered
- Intelligent
- Driven
- Values Quality Time

Although my emotions were not running wild initially, I knew that Daniel was a good thing in my life. After Daniel forgave me and we began dating again, my feelings for him quickly grew. The more I was around Daniel and learned about him, the more I liked him. He also happened to be incredibly handsome and he treated me like a princess. When my emotions came into play, it was like a snowball effect. They grew and grew with increasing velocity.

After he met my family, they all expressed to me that they absolutely loved him. My family is such a big part of my life. It made me happy beyond words that they liked him so much. But even more importantly, I loved talking to him and us spending time together. It took about a month for me to realize I wanted to be his girlfriend. This was a huge victory in overcoming my past and being afraid of commitment. However, Daniel liked to take things slow, and it took a little more time for us to become official. Two months into the relationship was when he asked me. When he asked, I could tell that he was nervous, and it was really cute. The fact that he chose not to dive into a relationship and that he waited to ask me until we had established a solid foundation built on friendship and trust made me understand that he meant what he was asking. It also made me being his girlfriend feel like such a privilege. I felt so special and incredibly blessed. As Daniel and I continue dating, it is my prayer that Christ will always be at the center of our relationship.

After the flood, God made a promise to Noah that He would never flood and destroy the earth again. God established a covenant and created the rainbow to signify His promise. Seek God in prayer and establish a covenant between you and the Lord. Ask that He would guide, protect, and strengthen you in your walk with Jesus Christ. In whatever season of life you are currently in, live in such a way that pleases God. Living life in full pursuit of Jesus will honor God and will attract the type of man you are looking for. To attract a man that is a Christian leader, you must become just that, a Christian leader! To attract someone who is trustworthy and caring, you must practice these things yourself. Be the right kind of bait. Using the wrong kind of bait will only attract a fish that you will need to throw back anyways.

Never ever settle for less than God's best. Single, Christian men who are spiritual leaders and live sold out lives for Christ are out there! Just don't get caught up looking in all of the wrong places, dating the wrong people, or doing the wrong things. You won't find godly men in sinful circumstances.

In the meantime, stop searching. Be patient. Set your standards high, and strengthen your relationship with Christ. Give up striving to find that person to fulfill you, and first allow Jesus to meet your every need and complete your life. Give God the pen to write your love story.

THE GREAT HEALER

Just then a woman who had been subject to bleeding for twelve years came up behind him and touched the edge of his cloak. She said to herself, "If I only touch his cloak, I will be healed." Jesus turned and saw her. "Take heart daughter," he said, "your faith has healed you."
— Matthew 9:20-22

In this Bible story, a woman who had been bleeding for twelve years came to Jesus with unwavering faith. She knew that if she could only touch Jesus' cloak that her wound would be healed. Because of the woman's faith, Jesus healed her wound. In the same way, we are called to take heart and have faith in Jesus that He will heal our hurt. For this reason, we will not place our faith in other men, being skinny, significance, or material goods! These things may be temporary Band-Aids, but the wound will be fully healed only when we place our hope and full confidence in God, the Great Healer.

BEING "NEEDY"

Have you ever known a girl or had a friend who was constantly in need of your help and advice? We all know of someone who fits this description. Maybe you are thinking, *That person is me!* At this time in your life, coming out of a difficult breakup, this person very well could be you, and nothing is wrong with that. Being surrounded by Christian friends who are always willing to lend an ear and give sound advice is so important, especially right now. But at some point, don't you want to be able to return the favor?

Finding your identity in Christ is the first step to becoming okay. This entails making cognizant decisions to make the intentional moves necessary to strengthen your faith. Setting aside a daily quiet time, finding a church, getting more involved in your church, seeking God in prayer—these are all excellent options for using Christ as the backboard during your rebound.

Maybe God is calling you to go on a mission trip. There's no better time than now to fulfill His plans. It is possible, that there's no better way to go about resolving your sadness than by focusing on helping others rather than focusing on your hurt.

The point is that we need to work on constantly being prepared to be a blessing to those in need. Our God is an awesome God. Seek His healing and the Lord will provide. Live in faith, and become the woman that God has intended for you to be.

STEPS TO BECOME THE WOMAN GOD INTENDS FOR YOU TO BE:

1. Find your identity in Christ - Accept Jesus into your heart. Ask Him to become the Lord and Savior of your life.

2. Strengthen your relationship with Him - Fill up your spiritual tank with God's Word, and learn about the nature of Christ from other Christ followers.

3. Listen for His calling - What is something that you know God wants you to do right now?

4. Carry out His calling - Execute the task God has placed upon your heart.

5. Become a blessing to others - Be a positive influence. Serve and help people with your hands, time, and listening ears every day.

Sometimes I wonder and ask myself the question, *Am I the kind of woman I want my daughter to be?* This is powerful question that forces me to consider my actions, choices, and lifestyle in general. *Am I doing the right thing? Am I making the right decisions for my life? Am I seeking God in prayer?*

There are several things that I'd like to change about my life that would improve my relationship with Christ. I'd like to read the Bible more. I'd like to be more consistent with having quiet times. I'd like to be more of a prayer warrior.

One time during Bible study, I had to use the bathroom. I noticed there was a Post-it note on the mirror, with a scribbled-out question. *Am I talking about it more than I am praying about it?* This question really shifted a gear inside of me. It forced me to look inward, and to consider my motives and intentions. Am I truly praying about it more than I am ranting on to others about it, and gossiping about it? Oftentimes, the answer is sadly no.

No matter what "it" is, I have to deliberately pray about my concerns, and present my petitions to God before I express them to people. The reason why this is so hard for me to do is because I often lose focus on Christ. My focus shifts to things other than Jesus—things that can give me an easy answer or instant gratification, especially things such as people's opinions.

It's easy to fall into this trap, but I fall into grace. Each day is a new day, and Christ offers forgiveness. By developing a consciousness and a mind-set that is focused on pleasing and relying on Jesus, I can do a 180 with these bad habits. Over time, I can change from a people pleaser into a prayer warrior. (People pleasing will be discussed more in later chapters.) A prayer warrior is a person who engages in spiritual warfare by praying for others consistently and effectively according to the Bible. To become prayer warriors, we must fight the good fight and put on the full armor of God (Ephesians 6:10-18).

And pray in the Spirit on all occasions with all kinds of prayers and requests. With this in mind, be alert and always keep on praying for all the Lord's people.
— Ephesians 6:18

A lady named Molly taught me how to pray when I was a freshman in college. She taught me that there are four parts to prayer: 1. praise; 2. thanksgiving; 3. forgiveness; and 4. prayer requests. These four components enable me to have a better relationship with Jesus Christ through prayer.

THE FOUR COMPONENTS OF PRAYER

1. Praise: The first part of prayer is praise. Praise God for His awesome power. Praise God that He is the Creator of the universe. Praise God that He is infinite and full of mercy.

2. Thanksgiving: Thank God for all of the blessings and opportunities that He has placed in your life. Thank God for sending His only son to die on the cross to take away our sins.

3. Forgiveness: Seek God's forgiveness. Speak to Jesus about the specific ways that you have sinned, and ask Him to change the conditions of your heart and redirect your motives. Asking for His forgiveness is an essential component of prayer.

4. Prayer Requests: Ask for God's help in a specific way. Ask for God's healing and restoration in all circumstances.

Praying these four components in this specific order helps me to shift the focus of my life from me to God. This order allows me to put my trust in God by first realizing how wonderful He truly is, recognizing His many blessings in my life, remembering Jesus' ultimate sacrifice, addressing and confessing my sins to God, and lastly, asking for God to grant the specific needs in my life. It is hard for me not to petition my requests to God initially in prayer, but by recognizing the essence of God's steadfast love and grace first, my perspective is changed and my heart is softened to the Potter's hands.

PRAYER:

You are amazing God. You are The Almighty Creator of the universe. Your name is holy, mighty, and worthy of praise. You are the Prince of Peace and Lord of lords. God, You are my glory.

Thank You for sending Your son, Jesus, to die on the cross to take away my sins. Thank You for my supportive family, my sweet friends, a job that I enjoy, an inviting church, and for this wonderful season in my life. Thank You, Lord, for Your many blessings!

I pray that You would forgive me for my selfish ambitions and wrong motives. Jesus, forgive me and take away these sins. Help me to place the needs of others before myself. Help me to give You the glory in all things. Jesus, fill me with the Holy Spirit. Guide me in Your truth, direct me in all of my ways, and forgive me when I stumble and sin.

I pray that You would heal my great-grandmother after her surgery, Lord, and help her to fully recover. I pray that you would help me in school. Help me to stay motivated and give it my all. I pray that You would show me your will for my life in future job opportunities. I love You and need You, Jesus. Amen.

CHAPTER TEN

P31 WOMEN

THE WIFE OF NOBLE CHARACTER
(PROVERBS 31:10-31)

A wife of noble character who can find?
She is worth far more than rubies.

Her husband has full confidence in her
and lacks nothing of value.

She brings him good, not harm,
all the days of her life.

She selects wool and flax
and works with eager hands.

She is like the merchant ships,
bringing her food from afar.

She gets up while it is still night;
she provides food for her family

and portions for her female servants.
She considers a field and buys it;

out of her earnings she plants a vineyard.
She sets about her work vigorously;

her arms are strong for her tasks.
She sees that her trading is profitable,

and her lamp does not go out at night.
In her hand she holds the distaff

and grasps the spindle with her fingers.
She opens her arms to the poor

and extends her hands to the needy.
When it snows, she has no fear for her household;

for all of them are clothed in scarlet.
She makes coverings for her bed;

she is clothed in fine linen and purple.
Her husband is respected at the city gate,

where he takes his seat among the elders of the land.
She makes linen garments and sells them,

and supplies the merchants with sashes.
She is clothed with strength and dignity;

she can laugh at the days to come.
She speaks with wisdom,

and faithful instruction is on her tongue.
She watches over the affairs of her household
and does not eat the bread of idleness.

Her children arise and call her blessed;
her husband also, and he praises her:

"Many women do noble things,
but you surpass them all."

Charm is deceptive, and beauty is fleeting;
but a woman who fears the Lord is to be praised.

Honor her for all that her hands have done,
and let her works bring her praise at the city gate.

WHAT DOES IT MEAN TO be a Proverbs 31 Woman? Most think that this means being a godly woman and a supportive wife. While this is true, digging deeper into this chapter of Proverbs, we find that a P31 woman encompasses so much more.

The words capable, intelligent, virtuous, hardworking, and precious to her husband are all accurate descriptions. A P31 woman is confident in herself and her identity in Christ. She is trustworthy. She provides for her family and is not lazy. The conditions of her heart are pure. A P31 woman encompasses the fruits of the Spirit: love, joy, peace, patience, kindness, goodness, faithfulness, gentleness, and self-control. She is her husband's biggest cheerleader, his number one fan. She constantly encourages, comforts, and supports him in all of his endeavors. In turn, he is extremely proud of her, and admires her for her strength of character. A P31 woman is a rock-star mom. She nurtures her kids, and provides them with food and clothing. They love her dearly. Her reputation is that of dignity by all who know her. Thinking about the future is exciting to this woman because she knows that God has great things in store! Most importantly, a P31 woman's beauty and self-worth does not amount to how pretty she is on the outside, but rather her beauty relies on her love for Jesus Christ and the conditions of her heart.

Charm is deceptive, and beauty is fleeting; but a woman who
fears the Lord is to be praised.
— Proverbs 31:30

We all know a P31 woman. Although they are rare, we all know at least one. Think about the P31 woman that is in your life. What is it about her that is different, and sets her apart as P31 quality?

My colleague and friend, Katelyn, is a P31 woman. We worked together for a year in college as graduate teaching assistants. I learned a lot from Katelyn. Although she was incredibly wise as a woman of God, I learned not by her words, but rather her actions, by the way she lived her life. Katelyn was patient, gentle, quiet spirited, and she feared the Lord. Instead of listening to worldly messages, and placing other interests before her relationship with Christ, she cared more than anything else about what Jesus thought of her actions and intentions. Jesus was number one in Katelyn's heart and her actions and attitudes reflected this truth. She found her identity in Christ—living for Him, and loving others. Her fear and love for her personal Lord and Savior, Jesus Christ, was worn like a badge of honor.

Katelyn went against the grain. "Going against the grain" is often associated with a negative connotation, but in all reality, Katelyn was a light in my life and a blessing to all who knew her. She was like a mirror facing the sun. She absorbed the light and love of Jesus and exuded His brilliance on everyone she came into contact with.

Katelyn is going to heaven someday and is bringing others with her. One of the most astounding attributes of this friend and sister in Christ was that she was intentional about sharing the gospel. Katelyn is responsible for impacting the life of another friend of ours, Emily, whom she led back to Christ and back to church. While she is one of the most humble persons I know, I am certain there are other accounts that I am unaware of where Katelyn established relationships with the lost and led them to Christ. She was always bold in her faith. Although Katelyn comes across as quiet and shy at times, she is not ashamed of the gospel of Christ!

I have a precious baby sister. Alison is right on track to becoming the woman God intends for her to be. She loves the Lord more than anything, more than anyone, above all else. Even when life throws its punches, Alison leans on the Lord for her strength and comfort. I look up to my little sister. I look up to her as if she was my big sister sometimes because of the way she lives her life. My little sister is someone who has found her identity in Christ at a young age. She is spiritually mature beyond her years. Alison doesn't care what other people think. My little sister is absolutely gorgeous, but she is also a Jesus freak who cares more about her internal beauty than her outward appearances.

Alison is a sophomore at Texas A&M University. She has made some lifelong friends through her sorority, Pi Phi. She values her friends, and the time they spend together. She chooses to actively nurture those friendships. Alison's friends are strong Christian women who support and uplift her. They go to church with Alison on Sundays, and even when they can't make it, Alison is a diligent enough person to go to church on her own. She brings her notebook, pen, and Bible every Sunday—and she takes notes avidly. Alison puts the pastor's sermons and God's Word into action. She not only hears the Word of God, but she also internalizes its messages and applies those biblical principles to her life.

Alison is not a spiritual consumer, but rather a contributor. She works every summer at a Christian sports camp called KIVU and leads high school girls to Christ. Alison strives to be more like Christ daily, but even when she does fall down and stumble upon sin, she seeks God's forgiveness, gets right back up, and continues sprinting toward the cross.

While Alison is experiencing so much joy, she is also learning about life and the nature of God through tough experiences. What I want most for my baby sister is for her to be happy, but even when she is not, she fully relies on the Lord for strength and healing. She runs into the arms of Jesus instead of running to the world to be embraced when she needs it the most, because she knows that only the Lord can make something beautiful out of life's ruins. Alison is a P31 woman.

PRAYER:

Lord Jesus,

By Your grace, Jesus, strengthen and guide me to become a blessing to others. Help me to live out Proverbs 31, the story of the wife of noble character. Fill me with the fruits of the Spirit. Reset my focus on living for You and leading others to Christ. Make me holy. Make me new. Purify my thoughts, words, actions, and intentions. Help me to become a P31 woman by strengthening my relationship with You, Jesus, and placing You above all else. I love You, Jesus. It's in Your heavenly name I pray. Amen.

CHAPTER ELEVEN

ETERNAL FOOTPRINTS

~February 7, 2004

For I am not ashamed of the gospel of Christ for it is the power of the Lord through salvation for everyone who believes.
— Romans 1:16

If you have a conviction about something, you believe in it 110 percent. Jesus Christ is my conviction and I want to live for Him and totally surrender my life to Him. I want to take up my cross and follow Him with all of my strength and all of my might. Amen.

WHILE CLEANING OUT MY CLOSET at home, I found photo albums, sketchbooks, diaries, and prayer journals from when I was a little girl. These old diaries and journals date all the way back to 1998, when I was seven years old. Finding these journals, where I had spent so many hours pouring out my heart, was like finding buried treasure. Reading through some of the entries reminded me that in Christ, we are to become like little children again. Children of God are desperate for wisdom and truth. Children of God are dependent upon Him for their every need. The words and messages of truth from the passages I read brought me back to the place of my childhood, a place where the song "Jesus Loves the Little Children" is constantly playing. I slipped back into that place of pure innocence of having a perspective of the world through untainted eyes—a place of sweet laughter and joy, a place where we are always forgiven and free. That's when I realized: my life still is capable of being all of these things. By accepting the free gift of salvation from the Lord, Jesus Christ, each one of our lives can be enriched with peace, love, and joy. By the power of the blood shed by Jesus, and through accepting this gift, we automatically become children of the Most High. Because we are forgiven and have been set free, we are able to look at the world with a fresh perspective, through the eyes of a child. No longer does the weight of the world, sin, reside upon our shoulders. Jesus Christ takes our burdens from us, and in return, we are to pick up our cross and follow Him to the finish line.

So in Christ Jesus you are all children of God through faith.
— Galatians 3:26

God does not refer to us as His adults. He refers to us as His children. If God is my heavenly Father, then I am His child. Being a child of God, and having a healthy relationship with my heavenly Father requires several essential parts, or pieces. If one piece is lacking, then part of the peace in my life will be missing.

1. Nurture - To care for and encourage the growth or development of. Do we welcome Him to nurture us? Do we rely on Him for the tender love and care that we so desperately need as human beings?

2. Affectionate, relational desire - To be delighted in. The sense that we are not just tolerated. "And so we know and rely on the love God has for us" (1 John 4:16). Do we know and believe God's love?

3. Apprenticeship - Accepting the parent's very self. Christ pours Himself into us. We are a dwelling place of the Holy Spirit—let's get in touch with that.

4. Exhortion - Instruction that comes from God. "For you know that we dealt with each of you as a father deals with his own children, encouraging, comforting and urging you to live lives worthy of God, who calls you into his kingdom and glory" (1 Thessalonians 2:11-12). The Greek word for exhort is "parakaleo." "Para" means to the side of, and "kaleo" is to call. The Father calls us to His side. Like a son works beside his father, learning the ways of his work, our heavenly Father instructs us to work and learn by His side.

5. Encouragement - To talk to and relate to someone. Do we allow God to cheer us up when we are running on E and need it the most? Is our daily inspiration coming from the Father?

6. Infusion - Spiritual charge. Sometimes God tells us, "Get up and do what I have called you to do!" There is a time to cry on Christ's shoulder, but there is also a time to dry those tears, stand up, be bold in our faith, and take action.

LEACHES

-June 11, 2003

Most teens are driven by the need for approval. Everyone wants to be accepted. No one wants to be the kid that sits by their self everyday at lunch. However, it is impossible to please everyone. Jesus said, "No one can serve two masters." Don't worry about what others will think of you. Think of what God will say in all your actions. Next time you go to the mall, think of what God would say if he was standing right in front of you as you try on clothes. Always keep in mind that some people are unpleasable in life. If you're popular, it's OK, just make sure it's for the right reasons. Those who always follow the crowd usually get lost in it. Be satisfied with yourself and your life. Do not waste your whole life trying to be the most popular kid in school. If you are controlled by the opinions of others, you are almost guaranteed to miss the purpose God has planned for your life. In heaven, having approval from everyone will have no meaning.

Although this journal entry was written when I was thirteen years old, its messages contain profound truths! My favorite sentence is, "If you are controlled by the opinions of others, you are almost guaranteed to miss the purpose God has planned for your life." Let this truth sink in. In order to step towards my destiny, I must first let go of the burden of my insecurity.

I have many insecurities: weight, appearance, intelligence, significance, income, self-worth, my ability to carry on a conversation, and my relationship status. These are only a few. People pleasing is the root issue of most of my insecurities. Sometimes, I strive to please others even more than I strive to please Christ.

I went out on date once with this guy, and he asked me what restaurant I wanted to go to. Because I liked the guy a lot, I didn't want to pick a place that he didn't like, so I told him that I didn't care. Throughout the night, he asked me a series of questions, wanting to know my opinion, to which I answered, "I don't know," "It doesn't matter," "I don't really care," or "I like them both!" I never voiced my opinion on any subject matter that went against his ideas or opinions, so he never really got the chance to get to know me. I was bummed when I didn't get asked out again, but there was a hard lesson learned: People don't like people pleasers! Learn to be yourself, stand out in the crowd, and dare to be unique, even if it means disagreeing with somebody else's opinion.

Along with every other insecurity, people pleasing is a like a leach—a filthy, blood-sucking parasite that has the potential to drain us of our fortified strength in Christ if we do not remove it quickly. It can also cause other harmful diseases, which can lead to a spiritual death. What is your leach?

The first journal passage, at the very beginning of this chapter, from when I was a little girl, rings innocence in the form of a desperate desire to please the Lord. Having this desperate desire to please God is the first step towards removing the leach, whatever your "leach" is. In addition to having this deep desire to please God, we must also have God-focused drive. It is sort of like testosterone for males, except it is for Christ followers, and it enables us to be bold in our faith and act on our innermost, God-pleasing desires. God-focused drive also allows us to see past the pressure of the moment. It reminds us that we stand for truth and what is right. We stand for Jesus Christ, who sacrificed everything for us. Because of this, we are to sacrifice all that we can to follow Him.

The last thing to remember is: Don't let it come back! Once the leach is off you, remember the steps you had to take to get it off in the first place. Insect repellent always helps. Reading the Bible, going to church, and having Christian accountability and fellowship are all ways that we can stay spiritually rejuvenated, and keep those leaches away from of us!

FAITH FIGHTERS

Like mustard, peaches, bread, milk, and virtually anything else found at the grocery store, as humans, we have a shelf life. On this earth, we are born, we live, and we die. Because this world is all I that I know, eternity is a difficult concept for me to grasp. I am no theologian. I won't even start to try and explain the concept of eternal life. Similar to eternity, there are many other concepts about our faith and life in general that I cannot understand. I have simply accepted the fact that I will probably never understand these concepts until I get to heaven.

Another definition of faith is trust. Faith is pure, whole-hearted trust. Faith is trust in its fullest form. The Bible talks about a faith so strong that those who possess such great faith do not have to see in order to believe.

> *Then Jesus told him, "Because you have seen me, you have believed; blessed are those who have not seen and yet have believed."*
> — John 20:29

As Christ followers, we are called to this standard of faith. We are called to *walk by faith and not by sight*. I know that this is a very broad statement, but by allowing it to seep deep into our souls, and applying it to the different branches of our lives, it can hold meaningful truth.

A common question that both believers and unbelievers ask is, "Why does God allow so much suffering here on earth?" Going through a breakup is an extremely challenging and difficult experience. Oftentimes, there are no easy answers or quick solutions to the pain. An overwhelming sense of despondency can drown out our joy and zeal for life, but only if we let it. We must learn how to become *faith fighters!*

On my knees, face down, on my bedroom floor, I cried out to God, *"Why, Lord?"* With no man in my life to love me and call me beautiful, I felt hopelessly alone. I wanted to know why I felt this desperate need to have somebody, and if this void would ever be filled. *Will I ever meet the right man, God?* I got no immediate answer. Later I realized that no instant answer is actually an answer in itself. *Wait.* God was telling me to wait. Sometimes The Lord allows tough things to happen to us that will help us grow in our faith and bring us back to Him. When God is our only source of hope in life, this is a good place to be. This type of situation demands we find rest and peace according to His terms. It brings us to our knees and serves as a reminder that we cannot make it on our own. We need the cross and our Savior's redeeming love. Without Jesus, the ever-present void within us will remain empty no matter what good things happen to us.

Through my singleness, I have learned how to lean on the Lord for my strength. I have assurance that I am beautiful and loved. This knowledge comes from God. Finding my identity in Christ has been a journey. He is teaching me, tweaking me, and refining my focus every day. I am content knowing that I am beautiful in His sight and that He loves me dearly. God has given me a peace about my circumstances.

Depending on God for everything is the sweet spot in life. Singleness can be a season that has the capability to move mountains, given one powerful ingredient: great faith. "Faith is the confidence that what we hope for will actually happen; it gives us assurance about things we cannot see" (Hebrews 11:1).

In order to step towards our destiny we must also step away from our security. Think about Jesus' disciple, Peter. Peter was the only disciple in the boat during the storm that was willing to step out of the boat to Jesus by walking on water. Peter trusted his Savior's voice. He had faith enough to attempt the impossible. Even when Peter began to doubt, Jesus saved him from drowning. All that Peter had to do was take that initial step of faith, out of the boat. Is there a step of faith that God is calling you to take?

For me personally, God was asking me to tithe. I was in a tight financial situation when I heard Jesus' voice calling me out into the wind and waves to take this step of action. I was substitute teaching for a living and finishing my Master's degree. I started giving 10 percent to God because of something my mother said: *"Remember that the money you earn was never really yours anyways."* What a profound truth! My money is not my own. It is by God's provision that I have money in the first place, and so I will give back to God what is actually His. Ever since I've started tithing, God has provided me with all that I need to eat, live, and pay rent. He has blessed me immensely in other areas of my life too.

When Peter heard Jesus' voice calling him out onto the water during the storm, he had enough faith to step away from his security, and out into the great unknown. He calls us to do the same thing. Your faith step is probably different than mine, but by taking it, we become obedient to His will. When we become obedient to His will, the door to many other opportunities opens. This is the when and how we discover our God-given purpose in life.

Peter began to doubt once he was out on the water and saw the great waves. Because of his doubt, Peter began to sink. As we take our initial steps of faith, the trick is to not look at the crashing waves that surround us. No, we must keep looking at Jesus, and listening to His voice to help us be brave. But even if we do begin to doubt, God acts as a shield to the righteous (Psalm 3:3). Through practice, our faith can graduate from baby steps to the point where we are walking and eventually running towards the cross.

How big is your faith? Think about this past week. What did you pray for? Were all of your prayers answered exactly when, where, and how you wanted them to be answered? If so, you most likely were not praying big enough, or challenging yourself in your faith. On a scale from 1-10, rank the current state of your faith.

1   2   3   4   5   6   7   8   9   10

Is there room to grow? I sure hope so! No one is a perfect ten, but by considering ways we can grow in our faith, we can grow closer to God. Write down two or three specific "faith goals," which are resolutions that will help rejuvenate your spiritual relationship with Christ, and in doing so will help to expand your faith boundaries. Here are my three:

FAITH GOALS

1. Read the Bible daily

2. Tithe (10 percent of my earnings)

3. More Christian fellowship! Engage in activities that are Christ-centered that will get me out of my comfort zone, help me to meet more people, and develop strong friendships that are based on Christ's love.

Remember this simple truth: As long as you have a safe outcome, or guarantee, you do not have great faith. You can either have faith or control. You cannot have both! We need to become faith-filled, mission-minded, all-in risk takers who are willing to bet the farm. We will not insult God by playing it safe, or place boundaries on what we think God can do. Through prayer, allow God to break down some of the barriers that are blocking your faith.

Christine Caine once did a great sermon series for LifeChurch.tv that was about carrying out our individual role in the body of Christ. Her message was delivered as a personal call to action for every Christian. The message was for us to stop striving as members of the body of Christ, wanting to be in the limelight, and instead, to start allowing God to use us in whatever way He needs.

Becoming the woman that I am intended to be involves making sacrifices. Oftentimes, these sacrifices are humbling experiences that shift the focus from myself to God. Too often, I try so hard to be seen or recognized that I either: a) choose to carry out some other role that receives more recognition, but is not my God-assigned role or b) I give up. This is a sad reality, but by listening for and carrying out my God-given role, I can help keep the entire body of Christ in balance. The anterior cruciate ligament (ACL) is the smallest of the four ligaments in the knee. Despite its size, it is the most important ligament that stabilizes your knee, and prevents injury. In regards to the body of Christ, if I am meant to be a pinky toe instead of a foot or a leg, then let God's will be done. May I listen to God's calling and respond faithfully no matter what. Regardless of the conditions or circumstances, despite any earthly recognition for my words or deeds, might I be faithful to the whispers of His calling. While carrying out God's will for my life, I will let my spirit rejoice all the more, knowing that my treasure waits in heaven (Matthew 6:20).

In order to leave eternal footprints, we must learn to be faithful and obedient even in the littlest of things. Sometimes God demands an initial small step or two that we may think is unimportant. Sometimes, this step is not the step we want to take, and therefore it is not a priority. Oftentimes, we want to take this great, big, giant step that can be noticeable to others. What if God is asking a small favor of you, one without any recognition attached? Would you take an initial small step of faith in order to leave an eternal footprint?

Be careful not to practice your righteousness in front of others to be seen by them. If you do, you will have no reward from your Father in heaven.
— Matthew 6:1

Rejoice and be glad, because great is your reward in heaven.
— Matthew 5:12

If our treasure for these unseen acts of faith is in heaven, then maybe these seemingly small, ordinary steps are the most important steps of them all. Perhaps it's the littlest steps of faith that have the power to impact others, and leave eternal footprints.

PRAYER:

With God all things are possible.
— Matthew 19:26

Lord, help me to remember this truth. Let my faith grow and become strong enough for me to move mountains in Your name, God. Enable me with the courage and wisdom to become a faith fighter. Break down all walls and barriers that are blocking my ability to have great faith. Lead me to the cross through strides of faith. In Jesus' name I pray. Amen.

CHAPTER TWELVE

THE KIND OF LOVE THAT WE DESERVE

Love can be expressed in so many different ways—a hug, a kiss, a conversation, a note, a laugh, time spent, a whispered prayer, a selfless gesture to a stranger, a smile, or a helping hand to name a few. I believe love can be shown to people we hold the closest and also to those we have never met.

The truth is, as believers, we have someone who loved us before time began, someone who made the ultimate sacrifice so that we could live. Romans 5:8 says, "But God demonstrates his own love for us in this: While we were still sinners, Christ died for us."

I can't even fathom this kind of love. The Creator of the universe chose you and me, even in our darkest places. He has loved us to live in Him if we will accept the love he lavishes on us through the free gift of salvation.

— Kelly Hall

GROWING UP, I STRUGGLED WITH being confident. Because I was insecure, I always felt this constant need to have a boyfriend.

At age sixteen, I went on my first date ever. William picked me up in his dad's Mercedes convertible and we went to my favorite little restaurant, Camilla's. William and I dated for about a month before he broke up with me for reasons unknown. As a result, my self-esteem and confidence levels dropped, and this experience only heightened my insecurities. I had only one other boyfriend in high school.

In college, boys started to notice me. As an incoming freshman, I got a lot of attention from guys. This was so different compared to my high school experience. Many boys thought that I was pretty, and being noticed felt so good. If only I had known then what I know now.

If only I had known that being hit on by a guy didn't mean you had to reciprocate. If only I had known then that kissing is a very special act of love and affection. If only I had known that by giving myself away bit by bit, I would suffer emotionally, and my spiritual wellbeing would be damaged. If only I had known that what I was doing was making my Lord, Jesus, sad. I was hurting the heart of God, and setting a bad example for unbelievers.

What I do know now is that God's grace does not come with a measuring cup. He lavishly pours out redeeming love and grace to all who ask. We have all sinned and fall short of the glory of God (Romans 3:23). Still, there is hope, *even for a sinner like me.* By grace we are saved; and this is not of ourselves, it is a free gift from God—the giver of mercy (Ephesians 2:8). Do I believe it is possible to make Jesus sad? *Yes!* There is a point where God says, "Enough is enough," and He disciplines us. But we are always redeemed by His amazing grace when we ask for forgiveness from our sins.

God is bigger than we think He is. His plans stretch beyond the grasp of our understanding. The good and the bad things that happen in our lives can be used to grow our faith. Everything is meant to bring glory to God. Our testimonies, our jobs, our hopes, and our dreams—everything in life glorifies God. Even when we fail, by grace we are saved, and this brings glory to God.

> *But he said to me, "My grace is sufficient for you, for my power is made perfect in weakness." Therefore I will boast all the more gladly about my weaknesses, so that Christ's power may rest on me.*
> — 2 Corinthians 12:9

This verse is from 2 Corinthians, which is a book of the Bible written by Paul. If you think that God cannot use you to share the gospel, then look at the apostle Paul's background. Before Paul became a Christian, he persecuted and killed many followers of Christ. Paul, called Saul at the time, wanted to demolish the Christian church entirely. What made Saul do a 180 turn around, changing His old ways, becoming an apostle, and devoting his life to spreading the gospel, was essentially his encounter with God. Saul experienced the presence of the Lord when he was on one particular excursion, traveling to a city to persecute more Christians. During this encounter, God audibly spoke to Saul, commanding him to change his ways and commit his life to Jesus. After Saul's encounter with the Lord, Saul was forever changed in spirit and in deed. He changed his name to Paul, took up his cross, and lived as a disciple for Christ. Paul eventually died as a Christian martyr, but not before reaching many churches and people with the message of Jesus Christ, the Messiah.

By having a heart after God's own heart, we may find favor in the eyes of the Lord. The Creator often strengthens the weak, humbles the proud, or changes the heart of the opposed to find and demonstrate newfound fortification and identity in Christ. God chooses those who may be considered unimportant by worldly standards, but because of their great faith, the Lord is able to do awesome things through them. This is an underlying message of the Bible. The weak become powerful Christian examples of God's love and forgiveness, demonstrating His power and furthering His Kingdom after they have an *encounter* with God. This is the keynote of the message. God is able to work through those who *respond* to His encounter with acts of faith and obedience, changing their ways and living for Him.

> *Repent at my rebuke! Then I will pour out my thoughts to you, I will make known to you my teachings.*
> — Proverbs 1:23

> *You see that his faith and his actions were working together, and his faith was made complete by what he did.*
> — James 2:22

I have a theory that God works the same way in the present day and age. The Lord may use small, even sinful people to make a huge impact for Christ. His power is demonstrated through their testimony and the apparent change in their hearts through their lives. I'm not saying that you have to be a perfect Christian. Every girl faces her own battles. But, let us encourage other people—Christians and non-believers alike. May we be faithful in our actions and live life trusting God, because He knows the desires of our hearts.

DEAR GIRL

-Phylicia

Dear girl,

I know what you're doing. I see you in your room, looking at the Holy Words. You disbelieve the promises because a voice tells you the scarred and broken don't deserve a second chance. You think good men come from a high and holy sphere, beyond the reach of the crumb-eaters and the robe-graspers.

But you've forgotten something. Good men are good by grace alone.

You feel so undeserving of a Godly love. You think that who you are dictates the hope of your future. But who you are has nothing to do with this, and if who you are has no bearing on your salvation, who he is has no bearing either. The ground is level at the foot of the cross.

You may think your story is too alarming for a good man to handle. You may think no godly man could love a woman with a past like yours. Listen: God's men are draped in the same unmerited favor that you are. There is no favoritism. There is no better-than. But there is hope.

Dear girl, good men aren't good because of what they've personally achieved. They are good because they are grateful for grace. Because they understand the depth and height and breadth of the love they have received, they strive to live that love as the men God made them to be. In loving you, God's man will reveal God's grace.

It may take time, meeting God's man. You have to choose trust instead of hopelessness. It's this testing-period we call singleness—a trial, really—that only becomes a gift when we see the strength God's given us through dependence on Him. God isn't using your past as His outline for your future—and neither should you.

Right now, in this singleness-trial, He's teaching you. Don't let Satan speak condemnation over a daughter of the Living God. Don't let him snuff out the lantern in your heart.

Dear girl, a good man will still want you, no matter what you've done. He won't want you because of your past or in spite of it. He'll want you because you're God's woman: the kind of woman whose attachment to grace echoes his own. He won't be looking for you to prove yourself. He'll be looking for a hand to hold in this walk toward eternity. Because to him, your love is the favor he didn't deserve.

I used to struggle with my self-worth. I used to think that I didn't deserve the kind of love that God has in store for me. There's a quote from a movie that says, "We get the kind of love that we think that we deserve." While I was dating my ex, this saying struck a funny chord in me, and made me feel uneasy. This was because of the fact that I was dating the wrong guy. I was dating a guy who was simply not God's best for me. Today, I know this quote to be entirely true. We do get the kind of love that we think we deserve, so it is time that we reevaluate our self-worth and recognize how precious we truly are.

The kind of love that we deserve is more than what we would naturally expect. Society has subtracted the standards of chivalry and God-intended love to mere physical attraction. While being attracted to your spouse is very important, these other components: same Christian values, being treated with the utmost love and respect, faithfulness in all situations, even when the going gets rough. These are equally important qualities of a marriage. Do not believe for one second the lies of Satan that say you are not worthy of this kind of love. Because according to the Bible, you are.

The story of Rachel and Jacob demonstrates the kind of love that we as women of God are supposed to hold out for. When Jacob first met Rachel he was captivated. After staying with Rachel's family for a month, he knew that he was head over heals for Rachel. He would do anything to have her hand in marriage. Knowing this, Laban told Jacob that in order to have Rachel as his wife, he must first work for him for seven years. "So Jacob worked seven years to pay for Rachel. But his love for her was so strong that it seemed to him but a few days" (Genesis 29:20). After the seven years were up, Laban pulled an unfair stunt and swapped his oldest daughter, Leah, as the bride. After Jacob was tricked into marrying the wrong daughter, Laban told Jacob he could marry Rachel only if he worked an additional seven years. He did so, and finally had Rachel as his wife. Jacob pursued Rachel for a total of fourteen years before she became his wife. He loved her so much that he was willing to do anything to have her as his bride.

Someday, I hope that a man will love me so much that he will do anything to call me his wife. For his sake, hopefully it won't mean fourteen years of toil and labor. (I don't think my dad is this cruel anyways.) But I do hope he values me and is willing to go great lengths for me to be his bride. In order for this truth to become a reality, I must become the kind of woman a strong Christian guy would want to pursue. I must live my life for Christ, and hold out for the man that

God has intended for me. Above all else, I must hold on to God's truth that I am beautiful, special, and worthy to be loved.

I am worthy of the best kind of love, the kind of love that is God-given. I know that I need the kind of love that protects, honors, trusts, and perseveres. I want the kind of love that keeps no record of wrong. I deserve the kind of love that rejoices with truth. I long for a love that never fails (1 Corinthians 13:4-8). God has intended Christ-like love for our lives. Believe this truth, and hold out for this type of love, because it is the kind of love that you deserve.

PRAYER:

> Dear God,
>
> Speak truth into my heart on this subject, Lord. Help me to remember that I deserve a Christ-like love in a future spouse. Jesus, thank You for Your perfect example of love. Help me to always remember and believe in my heart that I am worth it. In Jesus' name I pray. Amen.

CHAPTER THIRTEEN

YELLOW LEAVES

MY IDENTITY IS FOUND IN Jesus Christ. Together, may we rejoice in this season of our lives, living life to the fullest with the strength and guidance of Christ, our Lord and Savior. May He enable us to be happy, compassionate women of God. My prayer is that I would continue to focus on striving towards the cross more than focusing on the idea of marriage or a romantic relationship. God is my rock and my salvation (Psalm 18:2). I want to pursue God with a tenacious faith. I will strive to put Him first, because I know that by doing this, God will take care of all of the other minor details in my life. He knows my wants and my every need. His perfect plan always prevails. I will choose to rest in the peace of His promises. It is my desire to praise the Lord through every season and circumstance. "Rejoice in the Lord always. I will say it again: rejoice!" (Philippians 4:4).

Philippians 4:5 goes on to say: "Let your gentleness be evident to all. The Lord is near." When I looked up the definition for the word gentle, some synonyms stuck out to me that really nailed what it is to be gentle: honorable, respectable, well-born, kindly, amiable. What we are called to do as women of God is to be gentle toward others, in our manner and disposition.

> Do not be anxious about anything, but in every situation, by prayer and petition, with thanksgiving, present your requests to God. And the peace of God, which transcends all understanding, will guard your hearts and your minds in Christ.
> — Philippians 4:6-7

God is going to take care of us. We do not need to worry about our relationship status. If it is God's will, He will put the right man into our lives, and provide a husband in His perfect timing. In the meantime, what we are called to do is to guard our hearts and minds with the peace of God that is established through prayer.

> Finally, brothers and sisters, whatever is true, whatever is noble, whatever is right, whatever is pure, whatever is lovely, whatever is admirable—if anything is excellent or praiseworthy—think about such things.
> — Philippians 4:8

Setting our minds on things that are holy is pleasing to God. But this takes work. Filtering out the bad thoughts and thinking only about the good takes spiritual training. We must mentally train and practice residing our mind on things that honor the Lord. Training begins on our knees in prayer. Having a quiet time set aside each day to pray and read God's Word transforms my thoughts into positive, encouraging emotions that stick with me throughout the entire day.

*Whatever you have learned or received or heard from me, or seen
in me—put it into practice. And the God of peace will be with you.*
— Philippians 4:9

Verse 9 presents a challenge. "Whatever you have learned or received or heard from me, or seen in me—put it into practice." Everything that I have been taught about Jesus, I am supposed to carry out in my daily life. Twenty-four/seven I am to obey God. Not just whenever it is convenient or comfortable for me to obey. No, this verse says that I am supposed to put God's Word into practice all of the time. We are to apply everything that we have ever learned about the nature of Jesus Christ in to our lives each day.

I was blessed to grow up in a Christian home. My family went to church every Sunday. I attended a Christian sports camp every summer where we learned valuable lessons about the love of Christ. I know the Ten Commandments, and most of the other messages that are in the Bible. I've attended Christian women's writers and speakers conferences. I am in a Bible study. The list goes on and on. You could say that I have learned a lot about Jesus, and still, it is so hard for me to apply every single principle that I have ever learned into my daily life. It is a constant battle to obey God all of the time. But through Christ, there is grace (Ephesians 2:8).

Substitute teaching was a humbling experience. While finishing up my Master's degree, this was my job. I was highly overqualified for the position, but despite my education status, I was still being paid the going rate, and this was a wake-up call. What I've learned is that schools and principals don't care about your qualifications as much as they do your past experience. During the teacher interview process, the only question they want to know is, "Can you teach?" Can you use your teaching credentials to reach students, or do your credentials simply sit on a shelf? This is all that principals and school administrators want to know before hiring a new teacher. In a way, the same is true for my relationship with Jesus. He cares about the way I am living for Him and experiencing His love right now. Am I applying what I know about the Bible, God's grace, and God's love to my daily life, or are my credentials simply on a shelf for show? When it comes down to the end of the day, Christ doesn't care about our "Christian credentials." He cares about the conditions of our hearts—how we are applying our knowledge of the nature of Christ to our everyday lives.

And the God of peace will be with you.
— Philippians 4:9

The end of verse 9 seals the deal. It leaves us with a reassuring promise. By setting our minds on God-honoring truths, an overwhelming sense of heavenly peace will consume our hearts and souls, and will pour out into our daily lives. This is our hope. This is our joy.

AMANDA

Amanda's life mission was to spread the good news of our source of hope that is found in Jesus Christ. Given her circumstances, Amanda should have been hopeless. She was diagnosed with stage-four ovarian cancer and the doctors had predicted that she had a year left here on this earth.

Amanda had a joyful spirit. Despite her cancer, she continued to be a missionary in Africa, educating the people of Zambia about Jesus. She did this with so much love in her heart. Her zeal for the Lord was evident, and she impacted the lives of so many.

Amanda proceeded to spread the message of hope found in Jesus Christ up until her last few moments here on this earth. Her final parting moments were spent praying for people, and speaking truth into their lives. Amanda's final prayer was that a multitude of people would continue on with her life mission: to spread the message of hope found in Jesus Christ to the world.

Something in my heart melted when I heard Amanda's story. While she remained joyful throughout her cancer, up until her last days, I so often become unhappy and self-focused when faced with a small problem. When the going gets rough, I often find myself questioning God's authority, asking these questions: *Why is this bad thing happening to me? Does God really know what He is doing?* The answer is a resounding yes. Regardless of audibly hearing God's voice or even sensing His presence, the answer is yes, yes He does. He is the guiding force through the thick and thin. We don't have to ask for a sign or a miracle to help us in difficult situations because God has already given us answers. The Bible provides the answer to our questions. The Word of God has the ability to weave truth into any situation. Maybe it is through a parable, or maybe God's will is more direct for you. In all things, the Bible is the source of our truth and hope found in Jesus Christ.

HEAVEN: THE REAL HAPPILY EVER AFTER

*When the perishable has been clothed with the imperishable,
and the mortal with immortality, then the saying that is written will
come true: "Death has been swallowed up in victory."*

*"Where, O death, is your victory?
Where, O death, is your sting?"*

*The sting of death is sin, and the power of sin is the law. But
thanks be to God! He gives us the victory through our Lord Jesus Christ.*

*Therefore, my dear brothers and sisters, stand firm. Let nothing
move you. Always give yourselves fully to the work of the Lord, because you know that your labor in the Lord is not in vain.*
— 1 Corinthians 15:54-58

May we stand firm on these truths: Our chains are gone. The sins
of our past have been conquered through the blood of Christ. Living
for Jesus, and spreading the good news here on this earth is not in
vain. Death has lost its sting. Because of His amazing grace, I have the
hope of heaven. Thanks be to God. His love endures forever.

*But the fruit of the Spirit is love, joy, peace, patience, kindness,
goodness, faithfulness, gentleness and self-control.*
— Galatians 5:22-23

In the Bible, joy is listed as the second fruit of the Spirit. Sometimes
I wonder if God listed these spiritual fruits in priority order. If God did
rank these fruits, joy must be important to our health and wellbeing. As
Christ followers we are called to "be joyful always" (1 Thessalonians 5:16).
So often girls (myself included) idolize the idea of marriage, placing it

on a pedestal that is smack dab right in the way of our happiness. Yes, placing marriage on a pedestal is dangerous because it can actually take away from our momentary happiness. We become so focused on reaching our marriage goals that our joy is compromised.

Before I meet my two, I want to already be living a lifestyle that brings glory to The One. After reading *Love, Sex, and Happily Ever After*, a book by Pastor Craig Rochelle, a great piece of advice really stuck with me. The advice was to focus more on preparing for a phenomenal marriage, than planning for a beautiful wedding. Thinking about my wedding day comes naturally for me, but I know that preparing my heart and my life for marriage, before I meet my husband, is essentially important to my happily ever after. Weaving a lifestyle and developing habits that are God honoring, healthy, and conducive to happiness begins way before marriage. Life doesn't begin when you meet your spouse. It begins when you accept Jesus into your heart as your personal Lord and Savior. Strengthening my relationship with Christ and living in a way that is pleasing to the Lord is crucial to attracting a godly man. Preparing for a marriage built on the rock solid foundation of God's love is dependent on Christ's current role in my life. Before entering into a romantic relationship, I must consider the wellbeing of my relationship with Christ. A marriage with a man ends at "death do us part," but a relationship with Jesus Christ is for all of eternity.

> . . . He will wipe away every tear from their eyes; and there will no longer be any death; there will no longer be any mourning, or crying, or pain; the first things have passed away. And He who sits on the throne said, "Behold, I am making all things new."
>
> — Revelation 21:4-5a NASB

Someday I want to be in heaven, praising God for all of eternity, but I don't deserve God's love. I really don't. Not even an ounce. I am a sinner, born with the need of a Savior.

His love is deep. His love is wide. His love is holy, mighty, and powerful. Words alone cannot cover the expanse of God's love. Because God loved me so much, He sent His only son, Jesus, to die on a cross, the most terrible death, to take away the sins of the world. This is the greatest act of love known to mankind. It is because of Jesus' death and resurrection that I have the hope of a happily ever after someday in heaven.

I can only imagine when I am in the presence of the Lord, standing at the foot of the throne. Will I dance, will I laugh, will I cry, will I sing songs of worship, or in awe will I just be still? I can only imagine what heaven will be like.

There are many theories about what eternity in heaven will be like. Some say the streets are paved with gold. Others think of heaven being a state of all of their favorite things on earth existing together, all at once. According to the movie *A Little Princess*, in heaven there are seas of thousands of wild sunflowers that shine brilliantly in the sun. While I hope all of these things are true, almost everyone I know agrees that there will be no more pain or sorrow. There will be no more tears. World hunger, lack of clean drinking water, cancer, obesity, and depression—suffering will not exist in heaven.

I have a theory of my own. My mom's friend, Mrs. Cook, once told me about the most special day of her life. In a sea of hundreds of smiling faces, every person who was there, she knew. The bride wore a beautiful white silk ball gown that was ornately decorated with delicate lace. Everyone on the scene was rejoicing. With tears of joy in her eyes, the bride slowly proceeded down the aisle. A sensation of excitement and euphoric bliss consumed her as she walked gracefully, with a sense of purpose toward her bridegroom, whom she dearly loved.

I think that entering the gates of heaven will be similar to a beautiful wedding. We will be meeting Jesus face to face, for the very first time. Many joyful persons, or spirits, we know will be there to greet us at this grand celebration. I think the main difference between an earthly versus a heavenly wedding is that instead of the bride being the center of attention, it will be all about the Bridegroom, our Lord and Savior, Jesus Christ. The wedding will be all in His honor.

This is what we have to look forward to. Even though Jesus' love and sacrifice is not the kind of love that we deserve, it is the kind of love that Jesus offers to us as a free gift of salvation. To all who accept, infinite love is the kind of love that we are granted. This means, Jesus is going to love us no matter what. And once we've accepted this gift, there's no place that we can run to, or hide to escape from His presence. There's no depth to which we can fall where He cannot reach us. Nothing can separate us from the love of Jesus Christ.

In the Bible, it talks about how a man is supposed to love his wife like Jesus loved the church (Ephesians 5:25). This is a very powerful statement, and while some things in the Bible I don't think were meant to be literal, I think these words were. If Christ loved the church so much that He was willing to give His life away, so that we might truly live, then this is the standard husbands are called to. So when looking, keep this in mind: enduring, steadfast, Christ-like love is the kind of love that we deserve. In the same way, wives are called to live for Christ by setting examples of purity, and to respect their husbands (1 Peter 3:1-2).

> Wherever you may be this very day and whoever you are with, I hope you know you are loved. Because you are. Very much. Profusely. We all are. You are loved by the King. The Creator who loved us first and gave his life so we, too, could share this love shown to us with each step we take.
>
> — Kelly Hall

Through this season in your life, know one thing: you are loved. Your family loves you so much, and you are loved by your friends. But most importantly, you are loved by the Creator Himself! God made you, and has a plan for you life. He is holding out His hand and saying, "Trust Me." Take hold, and make the most of your time, and spiritual gifts. Find the joy in today, and rest your mind in the peace of tomorrow. Someday, you will look back at this time in your life, and you will be amazed at how quickly the leaves began to turn yellow, and the seasons changed.

PRAYER:

> Jesus, I love you. Help me to seek Your face through every season of my life. Give me resounding peace today, and hope for tomorrow. I pray that I would be joyful always, pray continuously, and have thanksgiving in all circumstances for this is Your will, God (1 Thessalonians 5:16-18). Through all of my struggles and the tough situations that I may encounter, open my eyes to see the unique beauty that can be found in all seasons that are spent in Your presence. In Jesus' name I pray. Amen.

ABOUT THE AUTHOR

"Alex" Savage grew up in Midland and Southlake, Texas. She attended high school at Southlake Carroll High. While Alex has consistently demonstrated a passion for writing throughout most of her life, it wasn't until Alex's senior year of high school that her spark for book writing was lit. Dr. Ludwig Van Otto, Alex's English professor, and editor at Franklin Publishing, encouraged Alex to pursue writing as a career because he considered her a talented author. This encouragement has stuck with her ever since, and she continues to write works that bring glory to God.

For college, Alex attended the University of Tulsa (TU) where she majored in Elementary Education with a minor in Creative Writing. Alex was on the TU cheerleading squad, and was a part of the Chi Omega sorority. During her summers in college, she worked as a counselor at Kanakuk camps.

Alex is currently taking classes to obtain a Master's degree in Math and Science Education at TU. While getting her Master's, she also works as a substitute teacher for Jenks Public Schools. Alex attends Life Church in Tulsa and loves being a part of her women's life group. Alex writes mostly during the summers and in her spare time when she is not studying, substituting, or exercising. After graduate school, Alex would like to be a third- or fourth-grade math and science teacher.

For more information about

Alexandra J. Savage
&
A Beautiful Season
please visit:

www.facebook.com/AlexandraSavageAuthor
www.alexandrajsavage.wordpress.com
www.alexandra-savage.wix.com/abeautifulseason
alexandra-savage@utulsa.edu

For more information about
AMBASSADOR INTERNATIONAL
please visit:

www.ambassador-international.com
@AmbassadorIntl
www.facebook.com/AmbassadorIntl